THE CAPE ESCAPE

Redefining Your Superpowers

Dr. Gigi Hamilton, Ph.D., LCMHCS

Copyright © by Dr. Gigi Hamilton
The Cape Escape: Redefining Your Superpowers

ALL RIGHTS RESERVED. No part of this book may be reproduced or transmitted in any form or by any means, electronic or mechanical, including photocopying, recording, or by any information storage and retrieval system, without written permission from the author, except for the inclusion of brief quotations in a review.

ISBN paperback: 978-0-9883412-5-8
ISBN eBook: 978-0-9883412-6-5
ISBN audio: 978-0-9883412-9-6
Library of Congress Control Number: TXu 2-421-383

Cover: Hafsa Ahmad
Layout and design: Joseph Okerentie, icra8Design
Editor: Tracy Johnson, Proof Your Point

Address where to get copies: https://www.amazon.com/

Printed in the United States of America
Printer: aandrprinting@comcast.net

DEDICATION

In the intricate weave of human experience, where every life is interconnected, I offer my heartfelt gratitude to God. For transforming my personal challenges into avenues of connection and empowerment, I am profoundly thankful.

This book is dedicated to the brilliant souls who left our world too soon—those who felt ensnared by life's complexities, seeing choices as distant echoes. To Claudia Allison Clayton, Cheslie Kryst, and Dr. Antoinette (Bonnie) Candia-Bailey: may your legacies continue to resonate, offering hope, insight, and the courage to face and reshape our challenges.

To the remarkable women who have enriched my journey—pillars of strength and wisdom—you have shown me how to navigate the ebbs and flows of existence, transforming burdens into lessons of resilience and self-discovery. Each interaction has been a thread in the fabric of my life; each lesson a knot strengthening our shared human connection.

On this day, filled with the memory of my mother's (Judy Hamilton) birth, I extend a loving embrace to my Aunt, Judy's twin, Joyce Hamilton, sharing a love that transcends the confines of time and space. To Delores Ragland, my namesake, you are a guiding light. To Donna Lewis, thank you for shaping the contours of my character and womanhood.

In memory of Beatrice Hamilton, Patty Hamilton, Aunt Eura Mae Ragland, Ollie Levesque, and the myriad of influential souls whose physical presence has faded—your spirits continue to weave through the fabric of our lives, leaving an indelible mark on the hearts you've touched.

May this book echo the shared symphony of our struggles, inspire a dance of transformation, and reveal the profound interconnectedness that binds us, urging us to interlace our own stories with courage, compassion, and autonomy.

ACKNOWLEDGMENTS

Your belief in me is a beacon of light that guides my way. To Kendall Hamilton, Nicole Bonilla, Kenya Hamilton, Lamont Taylor, Latonia Reid, Red and Tiger Reid, Patricia Hamilton, Olla Hamilton, Gina White, Carla and Ealious Jackson, Nikkitia and Marsona Jackson, Altamit Lewis, Kevin, Keith, and Keyante Hamilton, Eunique Shaw Johnson, Sonya Jackson, Roye and Yolanda Durden, Tony and Karla Goodloe, Annette Jones, Cynthia Isler, Latachia Heath Coe, Denise Polk, Kimberly Tamsett, Mark and Dr. Cori Costello, Dr. Dietrich Stewart, Kiera White, Dr. Cara Alexander, Noah Alexander, Drew Hickman, Tony and Nikki Rushing, Renee Bobb, Michelle Taylor, Valarie R. Brooks, Jeff Ragland, Caryn Baptiste, Myla Poree, Ken, Janine, and Chandler McIntosh, Nick and Brandi Riggins, Bartina Edwards, Esq., Lynn Leary, Esq., Argo Alexander, Marlene Gibbs, Esq., Dr. Sherry Hamilton-Latten, Michael and Pam Hamilton, Tabitha Howard, Carol Bailey, Angie Traylor, Belynda Goins, Tiffani Teachy, Elizabeth McKee, Lakeisha Temple, Nikki Findley, Dr. Caroll Lytch, Brian and Tammra Granger and the numerous cherished individuals in my life—your roles are immeasurable, and your presence is profoundly appreciated.

With deep appreciation and boundless gratitude, I acknowledge each individual who has touched my life and work. To Sonia McClean, Chad Neely, Ambrose Patton, Shavonne Sellers, Shuray Merriweather, Clarissa Manuel Diaz, Kelly Edwards, Caprice Lynn Prior, Tracy Alston, Lorinda Robinson, Channie Thomas, Patrick Burris, Jaqueline N. Parke, Ivonne Soraya Erion, Donna Frederick, Khalil Shakeel, Mary Blake, Vernita Stevens, Kristen Mackey, Demond Dearing Sr., Dr. Etinnie Burnett, Vic and Gelyne Bonilla, Sabrina Clark, Karmen Johnson, Author Stokes, Shawna Green, Bridgett Sullivan, Jabari Courtney, Carolyn Rudgley, Derick Gant, Bea Cote, John Clemmons, Cherilyn Carter, Doris, Brashea, and Lacresha Levesque, Alan and Valerie Amidon, Jarvis Simpson, Natasha and Dr. Carlos Todd, Marjorie Connor, my entire Leadership Charlotte Class 40 members, and the many others who have been steadfast supporters—I am endlessly thankful. Additionally, my heartfelt gratitude extends to all my clients who trust me to guide them on their personal and professional growth journeys. Your trust is the cornerstone of my purpose and mission.

To those whose names are not listed here but whose essence is interlaced with the very soul of my being, know that your influence is the silent harmony that complements the melody of my being. Your place in my heart is enduring, your support foundational, and your contributions invaluable, enriching the narrative of this journey beyond words.

May this book echo the collective strength, wisdom, and compassion that you all represent, inspiring others as you have inspired me.

TABLE OF CONTENTS

Introduction — 07

1. The Superhero Paradox — 10

2. Earning Your Cape — 33

3. The Success of the Cape — 47

4. Why Can't You Take the Cape Off? — 55

5. The Weight of The Cape — 72

6. When Your Cape is Tattered from Trauma — 81

7. Trying to Dress up the Cape — 88

8. The Cape as Your Kryptonite — 93

9. The Red, White, and Blue Cape — 99

10. The Cape Escape — 110

11. Healing from the Weight of the Cape — 123

12. Your Cape Redefined — 128

INTRODUCTION

In the journey of life, especially through the lens of women, the path is often adorned with challenges that test the very core of our being. My name is Dr. Gigi Hamilton, and I have dedicated more than three decades to understanding, supporting, and guiding women through the maze of their lives. My mission has been to guide women to paths that lead to growth, understanding, and empowerment, both personally and professionally.

The fabric of this book, *The Cape Escape*, is woven with threads of shared experiences, struggles, aspirations, and triumphs. While each woman's journey is uniquely her own, the commonality of our experiences is undeniable. This shared narrative is not just a coincidence but a reflection of the collective psyche of women navigating a world that often demands superhero strength while offering human constraints.

My fascination with superheroes since childhood, combined with my clinical expertise, has led me to explore the dichotomy that women face—the expectation to be all things to all people versus the realistic capacities of our human nature. This exploration is not merely academic; it is deeply personal. As a woman, I have walked in these stilettos, felt these pressures, and faced these choices.

In *The Cape Escape* you will find stories and reflections that may mirror your own experiences or those of women you know. This is intentional. It serves to highlight that, despite our unique journeys, many of us navigate similar struggles, often in silence, believing we are alone. My clinical experience has revealed this common thread, and I chose not to delve into specific stories in great detail to maintain confidentiality and respect for the individuals I've worked with. Instead, I present a combination of experiences, drawing on broad themes and emotions that resonate across individual stories.

This book is born from witnessing too many women reaching a point where they feel stuck, constrained by a perceived lack of options, with their quality of life diminishing under the weight of unmet aspirations and unacknowledged strengths. It is a call to recognize those moments, to understand that while the challenges are real, they are not insurmountable.

The Cape Escape offers not only insight but a choice—a testament that there is not just one path but many we can choose from. It is an invitation to begin a journey of self-discovery, to redefine success on your own terms, and to find strength in the shared stories of women who, like you, are the everyday heroes of their own lives.

Welcome to *The Cape Escape* where you are invited to explore, reflect, and perhaps find a piece of your own story within these pages. Together, let's embark on a journey toward understanding, empowerment, and the realization that the cape we seek is not one of invincibility, but one of resilience, authenticity, and the courage to be unapologetically ourselves.

Please study these pages of *The Cape Escape* with a heart open to discovery and with eyes searching for new horizons. May your reading voyage be as enriching and transformative as the stories that await to dance with your spirit.

"You are stronger than you believe. You have greater powers than you know."
– Antiope to Diana, Wonder Woman

CHAPTER 1

THE SUPERHERO PARADOX

Cassidy's alarm goes off while it's still dark outside. Her day starts in a rush, getting the kids ready and off to school, barely pausing to grab her coffee before diving into the workday. It's a blur of tasks, calls, deadlines, all juggled with the skill of a circus performer.

After work, she drives straight to her son's soccer practice, where she spends time dealing with work calls about tomorrow's meeting. The day doesn't slow down. She rushes home to cook dinner, finding just a few minutes to sit down before she and her husband argue about not having enough time together. By the time her head hits the pillow, she's already dreading doing it all over again tomorrow. Cassidy is living proof of what it means to wear the cape of "success" every day.

Cassidy's story is not unique. Many women navigate life by juggling multiple roles: caregivers, professionals, partners, friends, and community members. They manage these roles with a blend of strength, resilience, and grace, while often putting the needs of others before their own. This constant balancing act is performed with a smile, and it is a testament to their unwavering dedication and love. Yet, this exhausting pace is not sustainable indefinitely. There comes a moment for many when the balls begin to drop, when the fatigue sets in, and the realization emerges that wearing the cape of "success" comes at a cost.

As we step into Navigating Our Quest for the Unattainable, we dive deeper into the fascination of superheroes and what they represent to us. We explore the symbolic capes we wear, the roles we juggle, and the moment we find ourselves questioning if we can keep doing it all. This chapter is not just a reflection but a call to assess our understanding of our strengths, success, and the true power of vulnerability. It's time to unravel the superhero paradox and discover how readjusting our superpowers can lead to a more balanced, fulfilling life.

The Ongoing Allure of Superheroes

In the captivating realm of popular culture, superheroes have woven themselves into the very fabric of our lives. These extraordinary beings, with their awe-inspiring powers and invincible spirits, transcend the confines of mere entertainment. They become symbols of aspiration, vessels of our deepest desires, and mirrors reflecting the possibilities that lie within us. But what is it about these fictional champions that grip our hearts and minds so powerfully? Why, even as adults, do we find ourselves drawn back into the embrace of their stories, yearning to emulate their feats of valor?

To understand this magnetism, **we must first acknowledge that superheroes are more than just characters in comic books or blockbuster films. They are the embodiment of our most profound dreams and the champions of our innermost hopes. They stand as the epitome of human potential, representing the triumph of good over evil and the courageous dream of transcending our limitations.**

From the earliest moments of childhood, superheroes find their way into our lives. As wide-eyed youngsters, we wrap towels around our shoulders as makeshift capes, ready to take flight into the world of make-believe, where we are invincible, where the impossible is within our grasp. These imaginary adventures, fueled by the caped crusaders and masked avengers we adore, carry with them a truth that transcends the boundaries of fiction.

Take, for instance, the enchanting story of Maria, a shy and introverted child growing up in a quiet, unassuming town. Often overshadowed by her more outgoing peers, Maria harbored a secret known only to her and her treasured comic books: a deep love for superheroes. When she adorned herself with a homemade cape and mask, something extraordinary happened. She transformed into a confident, empowered version of herself, free from the constraints of her tentativeness. Through her affinity for these legendary figures, Maria discovered an important truth—that even the seemingly ordinary among us can possess extraordinary qualities within. This realization became a guiding force in her life, leading her to become a dedicated advocate for children's rights. Maria's journey illuminates the enduring allure of superheroes, demonstrating how their impact extends far beyond the pages of a comic book.

But it's not just the children who carry the torch of this fascination. As we grow older, the cape takes on a different form—metaphorical, yet no less potent. For many women, the cape becomes a symbol of invincibility, a cloak of unyielding strength that society, often unwittingly, drapes upon their shoulders. Consider the story of Sarah, a high-powered executive and a mother, who juggles the demands of her career while shouldering the emotional well-being of her family. To the outside world, Sarah is the embodiment of superhuman prowess, seemingly capable of handling any challenge that comes her way. Yet, beneath the façade of invulnerability, Sarah often wrestles with the weight of these expectations, fearing that any display of vulnerability would be perceived as a failure. Her story resonates with countless women who bear the invisible burden of societal expectations, a burden that can become stifling, overwhelming, and suffocating.

This book, *The Cape Escape*, was conceived and crafted to unravel the complexities of this paradox—the appeal of superheroes and the pressures they exert on our lives. It was developed to provide a sanctuary of understanding, a haven of empowerment, and a guiding light for women who navigate the tangled landscape of modern expectations. Through these pages, together, we will explore the multifaceted relationship between women and superheroes, dissecting the enormous impact these iconic figures have on our identities, aspirations, and the intricate web of societal expectations. We will journey together through stories of empowerment and resilience, of vulnerability and strength, and emerge with a newfound understanding of how to don the cape of our own lives, on our own terms, and with steadfast authenticity. In the pages that follow, I invite you to embark on a transformative quest—*The Cape Escape*—where we shall unravel the mysteries of the superhero paradox and, in doing so, find the power to redefine what it means to be extraordinary in your own right.

The Origins of Superheroes

Let's embark on a journey that takes us through the archives of human storytelling, reaching back to the ancient civilizations of Greece and Rome. In the timeless myths and legends of these ancient cultures, we encounter the first echoes of what would eventually become the iconic figures of modern superheroes. The tales of gods and heroes like Zeus, Hercules, Athena, and Achilles were not mere stories; they were the foundation upon which the concept of exceptional beings with extraordinary powers was laid.

These ancient mythological figures served as archetypal prototypes, embodying larger-than-life qualities and ideals that resonated deeply with the human psyche. The gods represented the epitome of power, wisdom, and immortality, while the mortal heroes embodied courage, valor, and the triumph of the human spirit over adversity. These archetypal characters transcended the boundaries of time and culture, speaking to universal themes and aspirations that were shared by civilizations throughout history.

As we progress through history, we come across another significant milestone in the evolution of superheroes—the emergence of masked vigilantes in the early 20th century. This era, often referred to as the Golden Age of Comics, witnessed the birth of iconic characters such as Superman, Batman, Isis, Wonder Woman, and Captain America. These heroes stepped onto the stage of popular culture at a time when the world was grappling with real-life challenges, including two world wars and economic hardships.

The appeal of superheroes can be attributed to their ability to contend with timeless themes that resonate with people across generations. The eternal struggle between good and evil, the relentless pursuit of justice, and the embodiment of heroism in the face of adversity are narratives that have captivated human hearts for centuries. These themes, rooted in the myths of antiquity and brought to life in the pages of comic books, offer a lens through which we can explore our own values, aspirations, and moral compass.

The superhero, as a cultural phenomenon, has transcended the boundaries of fiction to become an integral part of our cultural psyche. These characters have evolved from mythical gods and heroes to complex, multidimensional figures who grapple with the complexities of modern society. Through their accounts, we find not only entertainment but also a reflection of our deepest desires, aspirations, and the persistent quest for meaning and purpose.

In understanding the mythic roots and evolution of superheroes, you are invited to look into the major impact these characters have had on our collective imagination. We gain insight into why superheroes continue to hold a unique and cherished place in our cultural landscape, offering a timeless source of inspiration and a mirror through which we can examine our own heroic potential.

Superheroes as Archetypes

I want to plunge deeper into the interesting concept of archetypes and their intrinsic connection to the world of superheroes. Archetypes, as illuminated by the Swiss psychiatrist Carl Jung, are the ancient, universal symbols and themes that dwell within the collective human unconscious. They are the elemental building blocks of our shared human experience, etched into the very fabric of our psyches. Superheroes, in their multifaceted and awe-inspiring glory, encapsulate these archetypal figures, serving as modern-day vessels for the timeless ideals that have shaped our understanding of heroism, salvation, and the determined spirit of the underdog.

The concept of archetypes extends far beyond the confines of mere storytelling; it permeates our very understanding of the human condition. Jungian psychology states that these archetypal figures emerge from the depths of our collective unconscious to manifest in the symbols that spread through our culture. Superheroes, as models of these archetypes, take on roles that are deeply ingrained in our shared human experience.

Consider the hero's journey, a central archetype that finds its embodiment in the heroic exploits of characters like Spider-Man, Harry Potter, and Luke Skywalker. This archetype follows the path of a hero who embarks on a transformative quest, facing trials, challenges, and ultimately emerging stronger and wiser. These heroes reflect our own innate longing for personal growth and self-discovery, resonating with us on a profound level. Through our struggles and triumphs, we see echoes of our own journeys and the universal human desire for growth and self-realization.

Another potent archetype embodied by superheroes is that of the savior. Characters like Superman and Wonder Woman personify the selfless protectors who rise to defend the innocent and uphold justice. They represent our collective yearning for hope and salvation in a world that often seems plagued by darkness and chaos. These saviors serve as beacons of inspiration, reminding us that even in the face of adversity, one individual can make a definite difference and bring light to the world.

Furthermore, the archetype of the underdog finds its expression in characters like Batman and Iron Man. **These heroes, lacking superhuman powers, rely on their intellect, resourcefulness, and unwavering determination to overcome seemingly insurmountable odds. Their stories resonate with our shared fascination for resilience, the triumph of human ingenuity, and the belief that ordinary individuals can achieve the extraordinary.**

During our formative years, especially in childhood and adolescence, we find ourselves irresistibly drawn to these archetypal qualities embodied by superheroes. As we navigate the complexities of self-discovery and identity creation, these characters become more than mere entertainment; they become role models and sources of inspiration. The archetypal narratives they represent shape our values, aspirations, and our understanding of the world around us.

Through the captivating lens of superheroes, you are offered an important opportunity to gain a deeper understanding of the universal tales that resonate with our shared human experience. These narratives transcend cultural and temporal boundaries, touching upon the fundamental aspects of the human psyche and the prevailing quest for heroism, salvation, and the triumph of the human spirit. In exploring superheroes as archetypes, we embark on a journey that reveals the intricate threads connecting our individual stories to the grand tapestry of humanity's collective consciousness.

The Role of Superheroes in Identity Formation

Superheroes yield a transformative influence within the intricate process of identity formation, especially during the pivotal stages of childhood and adolescence. We open the doors to a world where the iconic figures of the comic book realm become more than fictional characters; they emerge as powerful guides on the odyssey of self-discovery. At the heart of this exploration lies the recognition that superheroes are not just captivating tales; they are mirrors that reflect the boundless potential within each of us. They offer an inspiring narrative canvas upon which individuals paint their own aspirations, dreams, and ideals. Through these personal anecdotes and stories, we highlight the remarkable journeys of those who have found an insightful sense of self and purpose through their deep connection to these iconic characters.

Picture Madeline, a young woman on the cusp of adulthood, who finds solace and empowerment in the stories of Wonder Woman. Struggling to navigate the complexities of societal expectations and her own self-worth,

Madeline is drawn to the Amazonian princess's unyielding determination and commitment to justice. Through her connection to Wonder Woman, Madeline discovers a fountain of inner strength and an incredible belief in the power of compassion and resilience. These lessons not only shape her character but also influence her life choices and the path she chooses to follow.

In the grand journey of identity formation, which is often loaded with questions, uncertainties, and self-discovery, superheroes emerge as guiding stars, illuminating the path toward self-acceptance and purpose. They embody the virtues of courage, integrity, and empathy—qualities that resonate deeply with individuals as they navigate the complex terrain of their own identities.

As we delve deeper into this idea, a resounding truth emerges: positive role models, whether they exist in the realm of reality or fiction, play an extraordinary role in shaping one's self-concept and life choices. These role models become beacons of hope and inspiration, offering a guiding light in the journey of self-discovery. In exploring the profound impact of superheroes on identity formation, we unveil a dynamic interplay between fiction and reality, where the boundaries between the two blurs, and the heroes we admire begin to reflect the heroes we aspire to become.

The Influence of Superhero Media

The emergence of superhero movies, television shows, and comic books as dominant forms of entertainment has heralded a seismic shift in the cultural landscape. These narratives, once confined to the pages of comic books, have transcended their origins to become powerful cultural touchstones that resonate with audiences of all ages and backgrounds. They've evolved from niche interests to mainstream phenomena, capturing the imaginations of millions and leaving an indelible mark on popular culture. Our journey begins by examining the evolution of superhero narratives over time. From the Golden Age of Comics to the contemporary era of cinematic universes, these stories have undergone remarkable transformations. They've not only echoed the societal norms and expectations of their respective eras but have also played an instrumental role in shaping them.

The rise of the superhero genre paralleled major historical events, including World War II, the civil rights movement, and the feminist wave. Superheroes have been more than mere entertainment; they reflect the hopes, fears, and aspirations of their audiences. The role of representation within superhero media is a theme that has gained increasing prominence in recent years. Superheroes have the power to transcend the fictional realm and impact our perceptions of gender, race, and identity. They can challenge and reshape societal norms, promoting inclusivity and diversity.

Consider the rise of characters like Black Panther, Wonder Woman, and Captain Marvel. These heroes have shattered longstanding stereotypes, proving that superheroes can come from diverse backgrounds and represent a multitude of identities. Their inclusion has not only inspired marginalized communities but has also challenged prevailing stereotypes, inviting a broader and more inclusive perspective on heroism. Representation matters, and superhero media serves as a catalyst for reimagining who can be a hero. Furthermore, the impact of superhero media extends beyond the realms of fiction, seeping into the real lives of women. As you engage with these narratives, you can find yourself emulating the heroes you admire. These stories become indicators reflecting the potential for heroism within each of us, regardless of our background or identity. The positive self-image fostered by this media can ignite a sense of empowerment and inspire us to take action, both in our personal lives and in advocating for change on a broader scale.

By recognizing the impactful influence of media representation, you will gain invaluable insights into how these tales shape your self-image, inspire inclusivity, and challenge the status quo. Superhero media emerges not only as a source of entertainment but as a force for change, inviting you to reconsider your preconceptions and to envision a world where heroism knows no bounds. In examining the multifaceted impact of superhero media, we uncover a dynamic relationship between fiction and reality, where the accounts we consume become a mirror reflecting the change we aspire to see in the world.

Breaking Down the Superhero Myth

I want to embark on an introspective journey into the paradox that lies at the heart of our fascination with superheroes. We stand in awe of their commitment to justice, their unyielding moral compass, and their clear-cut battles between forces of good and evil. Yet, as we peer through the lens of reality, we recognize that the world we inhabit rarely offers such simplistic clarity.

Our exploration begins with an honest acknowledgment of the complexities that define superheroes. These characters, while larger-than-life and embodying the loftiest of ideals, are fundamentally the products of fiction. They exist within carefully crafted storylines where conflicts are neatly delineated and resolutions are achieved with a sense of finality. Superheroes, with their iconic costumes and staunch principles, epitomize the archetypal struggle between right and wrong.

As we dive deeper into the analysis of these complexities, I encourage you to develop and nurture critical thinking skills. The stories of superheroes, while undeniably captivating, are constructs of imagination, designed to entertain and inspire. They are not roadmaps for navigating the tricky web of reality, where choices are seldom clear-cut and consequences are not always just. By examining the nuances and contradictions within superhero narratives, I plan to lay the foundation for a more discerning and mature approach to facing the challenges of the real world. I recognize that the allure of simplicity offered by superhero fiction is a comforting respite from the often bewildering complexities of our daily lives. However, this recognition is not a dismissal but an invitation—an invitation to embrace the multidimensional nature of our existence.

The real world is a place of ambiguity, where ethical dilemmas are not always resolved with a triumphant punch or a climactic battle. It's a realm where the boundaries between good and evil can blur and where shades of gray are more prevalent than black and white. Superheroes, in their fictional grandeur, serve as a mirror that reflects our longing for clarity amidst this uncertainty. I encourage you to navigate the contrast between the clarity of superhero fiction and the intricate realities of life. This contrast is not a contradiction but an opportunity for growth. It prompts us to engage in thoughtful reflection, to embrace the complexities of our world, and to approach its challenges with a more nuanced perspective.

In breaking down the superhero myth, I find not disillusionment but empowerment—a realization that while superheroes may not exist in the flesh, the heroic potential they symbolize resides within each of us. By facing the complexities of our world with wisdom, empathy, and a commitment to justice, we can become heroes in our own right, transcending the limitations of fiction to create a better reality.

Superheroes and Modern Gender Dynamics

Let's discuss how superheroes have played a pivotal role in both shaping and reflecting the intricate patchwork of modern gender dynamics. To do so, we must take a look back, deep into the archives of history, scrutinizing the portrayal of gender roles in superhero stories and tracing their evolution to align with the ever-changing societal norms that define our world. Our journey commences with an examination of the historical lens through which gender roles were portrayed in superhero narratives. In the early days of comic books and popular culture, gender dynamics were often entrenched in traditional stereotypes. Male superheroes, with their brawn and bravado, were cast as protectors and leaders, while their female counterparts were relegated to secondary roles as damsels in distress or love interests. These portrayals corresponded the prevailing gender norms of the time, reinforcing the idea that heroism was primarily a male endeavor.

As we progress through time, we witness a significant shift in the landscape of superhero narratives—a shift that parallels the broader societal changes in attitudes toward gender. These changes are brought to the forefront as female superheroes emerge, no longer content to be relegated to the sidelines. Icons like Wonder Woman, Captain Marvel, and Black Widow boldly challenge the traditional gender roles that once defined their predecessors. They stand as symbols of empowerment, capable of not only holding their own in battle but also leading with intelligence, courage, and grace. These characters represent a transformation in the perception of heroism, underscoring the fundamental truth that heroism knows no gender. Characters such as Storm, Jessica Jones, and Kamala Khan embrace their unique identities, demonstrating that heroism can encompass a rich spectrum of experiences, backgrounds, and cultural perspectives. They shatter the glass ceiling of superhero representation, inspiring audiences to celebrate diversity and inclusivity. By exploring these aspects, you gain major insights into the dynamic relationship between superhero media and the ongoing journey toward gender equality. The descriptions of superheroes serve as both reflections of societal change and catalysts for progress. They highlight the strides that have been made in challenging traditional gender norms and stereotypes, fostering a more inclusive and equitable world.

As we navigate this terrain, we are reminded that the power of representation in superhero media extends far beyond mere entertainment. It is a potent force for change, offering a glance through which we can envision a world where gender equality is not just a dream but a reality. I invite you to engage in ongoing conversations about representation, inclusivity, and the transformative potential of superheroes in shaping a more just and equitable society. In embracing gender dynamics in the superhero realm, we find a reflection of the changing world around us and an inspiring vision of what lies ahead.

Recognizing Vulnerability

It is imperative that I explore the concept of vulnerability and its significance within the realm of superhero narratives and the complex tapestry of real-life expectations. We venture into the depths of the human psyche, shining a light on the societal pressure to appear invulnerable and the far-reaching implications this pressure can have on individuals' emotional well-being. Our journey begins with an acknowledgment of the pervasive societal pressure to maintain an image of invulnerability. This pressure, often imposed by cultural norms and societal expectations, compels women to present themselves as unshakable and impervious to the challenges of life. These women believe that strength lies in the suppression of vulnerability and that exhibiting emotional resilience is synonymous with success. There is a hidden toll that the disguise of invulnerability can have on individuals' mental and emotional health. The ongoing pursuit of appearing unassailable can lead to emotional suppression, isolation, and the silent suffering of countless individuals who bear the weight of their struggles in silence. The consequences of this pressure are not confined to the realms of fiction but resonate deeply with the lived experiences of real people.

This exploration does not dwell solely on the challenges posed by the expectation of invulnerability. Instead, we emphasize the immense courage it takes to acknowledge and embrace vulnerability. Vulnerability, as we discover, is not a weakness but a fundamental aspect of the human experience. It is the recognition that every individual, including superheroes, carries within them a spectrum of emotions, doubts, and fears. Through the narratives of superheroes, we find that even the most iconic figures grapple with vulnerability. They face personal trials and inner demons, demonstrating that vulnerability is not a hindrance to heroism but an integral part of it. This recognition becomes a powerful message for you to understand that seeking support, expressing emotions, and acknowledging vulnerability are not signs of weakness but acts of bravery.

By encouraging you to recognize vulnerability as a fundamental aspect of the human experience, I offer a transformative perspective. It becomes a key step in breaking free from unrealistic expectations and fostering emotional wellness. It signifies the liberation from the suffocating pressure to maintain an image of invincibility and opens the door to authentic connections, resilience, and the pursuit of genuine well-being. In embracing vulnerability, you are invited to embark on a journey of self-discovery, where the acknowledgment of your own imperfections becomes a source of strength. Through the lens of superhero chronicles, we discover that the most heroic acts often emerge from moments of vulnerability and self-acceptance. In recognizing vulnerability as a shared human experience, I want to empower you to navigate life's challenges with authenticity and resilience, ultimately fostering emotional prosperity and a deeper connection with the world around you.

I am unable to talk about vulnerability without addressing the various forms of trauma that women may encounter and the unique challenges you may face when striving to fulfill the superwoman ideal. We will delve into the emotional and psychological toll that trauma can exact and how it intersects with societal expectations. Additionally, I will discuss the ways in which trauma can shape an individual's attachment style and influence one's ability to form and maintain relationships.

By shedding light on the fraying of the cape in the context of trauma, I want to offer understanding and support to women who have experienced similar challenges. Through narratives, insights, and practical guidance, my information given seeks to empower women like you reclaim your sense of self, heal from trauma, and redefine your narratives with compassion and resilience.

The Pursuit of Balance

It is impossible to talk about stability without embarking on a journey toward the crucial goal of achieving a balance between the often-overwhelming responsibilities of personal and professional life. We confront the pervasive, yet unrealistic, expectation that you must embody the qualities of "superheroes" in every facet of your existence, and we explore the toll this mindset can take on your well-being.

My exploration begins with an honest examination of the pervasive cultural story that perpetuates the idea of being a "superhero" in all aspects of life. This narrative, often fueled by societal pressures, insists that you should seamlessly excel in your careers, relationships, parenting, and personal pursuits, all while maintaining complete composure and endless reserves of energy. This places immense weight on your shoulders and can lead to feelings of inadequacy and burnout. The overpowering implications of the "superhero" mindset on individuals' mental, emotional, and physical well-being, and the relentless pursuit of perfection in all domains can create a steep toll, resulting in chronic stress, fatigue, and a sense of never truly measuring up. The consequences of this approach are not only detrimental to you but can also disrupt the harmony of your personal and professional lives. I did not create this book to discuss the myriad of challenges; this is a guide toward solutions and a roadmap toward equilibrium. I offer practical strategies for you to find that balance that makes sense for you—a balance that allows you to thrive both personally and professionally. I emphasize the importance of self-care practices and the necessity of prioritizing well-being as a foundational pillar of life.

One of the central messages conveyed in this book is the redefinition of success. Success, as we discuss, does not necessitate superhuman efforts or the continual pursuit of perfection. Instead, it calls for a realistic and holistic approach to life—one that acknowledges the multifaceted nature of existence and the ebb and flow of personal and professional demands. Success becomes a state where individuals can flourish in their careers while nurturing their well-being, maintain fulfilling relationships, and pursue their passions without succumbing to the pressures of perfection. The discussion encourages you to adopt a mindset of self-compassion, recognizing that it's not only acceptable but essential to seek balance, to prioritize self-care, and to acknowledge that no one is impervious to the challenges of life. It promotes the idea that balance is not a destination but a continuous journey—a journey where you can evolve, learn, and grow while honoring your own unique needs and aspirations.

By providing practical tools and strategies, you will be equipped to navigate the delicate dance between personal and professional responsibilities, fostering a more comfortable, fulfilling, and resilient life.

The pursuit of balance on your own terms becomes an empowering endeavor, one where you can thrive, embrace your humanity, and redefine your own path to success.

Reshaping the Narrative

The prevailing narrative of success and self-worth—one that often demands superhuman standards and relentless perfection must be challenged. We have to adhere to the transformative concepts of self-compassion and self-acceptance, recognizing them as essential components of genuine well-being. We need to redefine success on our own terms. We confront the societal pressures that compel you to measure your worth against unattainable standards, which often lead to feelings of inadequacy and self-doubt. The message resounds clear: success is not a set-in-stone concept; it is as diverse and multifaceted as humanity itself. The path toward self-compassion and self-acceptance as cornerstones of emotional contentment is a necessary journey. We cannot ignore realization that imperfection is not a flaw but a testament to our humanity. Self-compassion becomes the gentle embrace that soothes the wounds of self-criticism and the catalyst for personal growth. Self-acceptance becomes the mirror that reflects the inherent worth of you, independent of external judgments or unrealistic standards.

You are the architects of your narrative. The stories of your life need not conform to external expectations or societal norms. Instead, you have the power to craft narratives that align with your values, aspirations, and unique journeys. The emphasis shifts from seeking external validation to fostering an internal sense of fulfillment and purpose in your life. I want to challenge you to set achievable goals that resonate with your desires and aspirations. These goals are not rooted in comparison or competition but are shaped by a deeply personal understanding of what brings meaning to your life. In doing so, you regain power over your destiny, forging a path that is authentic and deeply fulfilling.

In reshaping the narrative of success and self-worth, I want to empower you to embark on a transformative journey—one where you become the author of your own stories, celebrating your strengths, accepting your vulnerabilities, and embracing the richness of your unique human experience. This chapter serves as a guide toward self-discovery and self-empowerment, lighting your path toward a life defined by authenticity, purpose, and a profound sense of fulfillment.

Healing from Superhero Syndrome

Our exploration of healing begins with recognition of the toll that striving for superhuman standards can have on your physical and emotional well-being. We confront the reality that the relentless pursuit of perfection often leads to burnout, chronic stress, and a pervasive sense of inadequacy. The consequences are not limited to your life, but the impact can and will ripple outward, affecting relationships, work, and overall quality of life.

I want to talk about the importance of breaking free from the cycle of perfectionism. Striving for unattainable standards create a dynamic where you have a tendency to disappoint yourself as perfection is unattainable, however, striving to be the best you can for that day and that moment is more realistic and this mindset allows you to embrace a healthier, path toward success. By doing so, you can rekindle your connection with your welfare and prioritize your physical and emotional health. Taking care of yourself is paramount, and I want to remind you that seeking professional help is not a sign of failure but a proactive step toward healing and self-compassion to assist in dealing with the lingering effects of the superhero syndrome.

The Power of Collective Action

Societal expectations and gender roles are not absolute; they are shaped and perpetuated by the collective consciousness of society. This realization underscores the significance of collective action in driving positive change. It highlights the power of you connecting for a common purpose, amplifying your voice, and challenging the status quo. Community support is a foundational pillar for change. Communities provide a safe space for you to share your experiences, seek understanding, and gain strength from your collective resilience. It is within communities that you can find solace, validation, and the courage to challenge the societal norms that have held you captive. Let's not ignore the role of activism in effecting change on a broader scale. Activism becomes the catalyst for transformation—a force that challenges the entrenched stereotypes, biases, and unrealistic expectations that have shaped our society. By participating in movements that advocate for more realistic standards and greater inclusivity, you become agents of change, inspiring shifts in cultural narratives. I want you to be a part of the broader conversation about societal expectations and its impact. It instills the belief that positive change is not only achievable but within reach when you unite for a common purpose. By actively engaging in conversations, sharing your experiences, and supporting one another, you become advocates for a more equitable and compassionate society.

Collective action becomes a manifestation of the belief that change is not the responsibility of a select few but a collective endeavor. It signifies the understanding that when you unite your voices, you have the power to shape a world where success is defined by authenticity, where inclusivity is the norm, and where societal expectations are aligned with the diverse and evolving nature of humanity. I want you to not only feel encouraged but inspired to become agents of change. You are officially invited to participate actively in the movements that challenge and reshape societal norms, fostering a world where you are free to embrace your authentic self and where the pursuit of success is not a solitary endeavor but a collective journey toward a more just, equitable, and compassionate society.

The Power of the Cape: Symbol of Invincibility

For many women, the cape takes on a metaphorical significance, symbolizing the expectation of invincibility in their lives. To illuminate this concept, let's review the story of Giana, a high-powered executive and devoted mother, whose life parallels the complex realities faced by many women today.

Giana's narrative provides a striking portrayal of the dual roles that women often navigate in contemporary society. On the surface, she presents herself as a paragon of strength and resilience—an executive excelling in her career while simultaneously serving as the emotional anchor for her family. To the outside world, Giana embodies the image of a woman who can handle any challenge with superhero-like prowess. Her solid determination and ability to juggle myriad responsibilities make her appear as if she possesses an invisible cape, a symbol of her seemingly limitless capabilities. However, beneath this façade of strength lies a sincere truth—a truth that resonates deeply with countless women who bear the invisible burden of societal expectations. **For Giana and others like her, it's as if they are wearing a metaphorical cape that symbolizes their ability to shoulder everything without faltering. The cape becomes an emblem of their perceived invincibility, a symbol of their determination to excel in all domains of life. Yet, as we navigate further into Giana's story, we uncover the hidden cost of this expectation of invincibility. The pressure to be superhuman and to maintain a pretense of unwavering strength can be emotionally and mentally stifling.**

The weight of these expectations often leads to a silent battle, where showing vulnerability is viewed as a sign of failure. Giana's story is symbolic of the broader struggle faced by women who feel compelled to live up to unrealistic standards, all while battling the internal turmoil of self-doubt and the constant fear of falling short. Giana's story reveals the common practice of women who tussle with the same invisible burden of societal expectations. It sheds light on the suffocating nature of this cape of invincibility, emphasizing how the pressure to be superhuman can become overwhelming and emotionally taxing. Her story serves as a poignant reminder that behind the façade of strength often lies a complex and vulnerable reality. It calls for a reevaluation of the expectations placed on women, and a recognition that true strength resides not in the smokescreen of invincibility but in the courage to embrace vulnerability, seek support, and redefine success on your terms.

The Paradox of Superhero Fascination

In this section I want to address the paradox inherent in our fascination with superheroes—a paradox that stems from the recognition that these iconic figures are fictional characters born from myth and imagination. Despite our awareness of their fictional origins, we find ourselves irresistibly drawn to the simplicity and clarity of the worlds they inhabit. To illustrate this dynamic, we introduce the story of Emma, a talented graphic artist who serves as an example of this dilemma.

Emma's narrative offers a poignant example of how our fascination with superheroes can endure across the span of a lifetime. She spent her formative years idolizing these larger-than-life characters, deeply inspired by their sense of justice and the clear-cut battles between right and wrong. As an adult, however, Emma confronts the complex realities of the real world—a world where choices are seldom black and white and consequences are not always just. The stark contrast between the simplicity of superhero tales and the nuanced complexity of real life becomes apparent. Yet, Emma's enduring fascination with superheroes is representative of a broader human longing—one that seeks clarity and simplicity in a world full of ambiguity and moral gray areas. It is a longing to believe, even if only momentarily, that good can always triumph over evil. This contradiction highlights the powerful allure of the superhero narrative, which resonates deeply with our innate desire for moral certainties and uncomplicated resolutions. The universal human inclination to seek refuge from the intricate and often perplexing nature of reality exists and is perpetuated by this paradox. Superheroes offer a respite from the complexities of life, allowing us to momentarily escape into a world where clarity and justice prevail. They become beacons of hope in a world that sometimes feels overwhelming and morally uncertain. Ultimately, the paradox of superhero fascination serves as a reminder of our yearning for simplicity and moral clarity, even as we grapple with the intricate realities of existence. It highlights the long-lasting power of these iconic figures to provide solace, inspiration, and a momentary respite from the complexities of the world—a testament to the ongoing appeal of superheroes in our collective imagination.

The Cost of Chasing the Unattainable

You probably have not given much thought to the extreme consequences that arise from the unrelenting pursuit of superhero-like standards—an endeavor that takes a significant toll on both emotional and physical well-being. To illustrate the high cost of such pursuits, we introduce the story of Jane, a dedicated nurse who stands as a great example of the challenges many women face when striving to embody these superhuman standards. Jane's constant commitment to excellence in her profession has led her down a path marked by sleepless nights, chronic fatigue, and an overwhelming sense of inadequacy. Her story serves as a reminder that the pressure to conform to these superhero standards is not isolated but pervasive, affecting the lives of countless women who find themselves on a similar journey. There are harsh physical and emotional consequences that accompany this pursuit. Burnout, stress, and anxiety emerge as persistent companions for those who push themselves to superhuman limits. The toll on one's well-being is undeniable, highlighting the dangers of giving into the notion that success and value can only be achieved through unattainable levels of effort and perfection. It becomes evident that this cycle of relentless striving, often rooted in societal pressures and the internal drive for achievement, needs to be addressed for the happiness of women everywhere. Every woman must remember that true success should not come at the expense of one's physical and emotional health. It calls for a reevaluation of the standards that society imposes and a recognition that value and worth are not measured by superhuman feats but by individual qualities, resilience, and the ability to embrace one's authentic self.

Ultimately, Jane's story serves as a powerful reminder that well-being must be prioritized above all else. It should encourage you to reconsider the sacrifices you may be making in pursuit of unattainable ideals. I urge you to be a part of a collective effort to break free from the cycle of insistent perfectionism. By doing so, we can create a world where women are empowered to define success, embracing a more balanced and fulfilling path that honors your unique strengths and well-being.

Chapter 1: The Superwoman Myth Unveiled
Reflective Questions

1. How have societal expectations influenced your self-image and life choices?
2. Can you recall a specific moment when you felt the pressure to conform to the superwoman myth?
3. What emotions or thoughts arise when you consider the possibility of living the superhero syndrome?
4. How has the superwoman myth affected your relationships with others?
5. What are the most significant societal expectations you've encountered in your life?

Exercise 1: Write a journal entry exploring your earliest memories of societal expectations and how they have shaped your beliefs and behaviors.

Exercise 2: Create a list of three specific actions you can take this week to challenge the superwoman myth in your life. Implement and reflect on each action.

"Always be a first-rate version of yourself, instead of a second-rate version of somebody else."
– Judy Garland

CHAPTER 2

EARNING YOUR CAPE

A Journey Shaped by Developmental Theory

Vivian was raised by a single father who championed both tradition and innovation. Vivian's early years were infused with a blend of old-school values and new-age thinking. This unique upbringing set the stage for her developmental journey, one that was as much about forging her path as it was about honoring her roots.

From her first steps into the wider world, Vivian navigated the terrain of trust versus mistrust with an open heart, learning early on to find stability in the love and consistency provided by her father. As she grew, the quest for autonomy during her toddler years was encouraged, with her father supporting her early expressions of independence and self-reliance.

Entering school, Vivian faced the challenge of industry versus inferiority, where her diverse background became both a source of pride and a point of contention. Balancing the richness of her cultural heritage with the desire to fit in with her peers, Vivian began to weave the complex layers of her identity, each experience adding depth to the cape she was slowly crafting.

Vivian's adolescence was marked by the psychosocial stage of identity versus role confusion. It was a period filled with questions, as she pondered the multitude of paths before her. Encouraged by her father to explore all facets of her identity, Vivian experimented with various roles, each trial and error contributing to her understanding of who she was and who she wanted to become.

The metaphorical cape Vivian earned through these stages was not merely a garment of achievement but a tapestry of her life's experiences, beliefs, and cultural influences. It symbolized her journey through Erik Erikson's developmental stages, enriched by the dual influences of her familial legacy and the societal context in which she lived.

Vivian's narrative, distinct and rich in its exploration of identity formation, sets the stage for us to reflect on the intricate dance between our development and the external forces that shape us. Vivian's story is a testament to the power of personal growth and the complex yet beautiful process of "earning our capes."

From the moment a girl takes her first breath and gazes upon the world, an intricate journey of self-discovery unfolds. This journey is intertwined with the theories of human development, particularly the construct of developmental theory, which illuminates how individuals evolve over time.

Developmental theory states that human beings undergo distinct stages of psychological and emotional growth throughout their lives. One prominent framework that is relevant to this topic is Erik Erikson's psychosocial stages of development. Erik Erikson, a towering figure in psychology, embarked on a captivating journey of self-discovery that paralleled his groundbreaking theories. Raised by a single mother in Germany, he grappled with questions of identity and belonging from an early age, an experience that deeply influenced his later work. His migration to America, where he studied under the tutelage of Anna Freud, daughter of Sigmund Freud and a renowned psychoanalyst in her own right, marked a turning point in his career, propelling him toward pioneering research on psychosocial development. Erikson's remarkable life and insights continue to inspire generations of psychologists and seekers of self-understanding.

According to Erikson, individuals face specific psychosocial challenges at different life stages, and the manner in which they navigate these challenges shapes one's identity. In infancy, the first stage is trust versus mistrust, where the infant learns to trust their caregivers and the world around them. The second stage, autonomy versus shame and doubt, occurs during toddlerhood, where children develop a sense of independence and autonomy. The third stage, initiative versus guilt, typically happens during the preschool years, as children begin to assert themselves more in social interactions. In the case of seven-year-olds, they typically fall within Erikson's stage of industry versus inferiority stage which occurs during the school years. This stage is crucial for the development of their own belief systems as they begin to explore their abilities, interests, and values, forming a sense of competence and self-esteem.

In the context of this section, the metaphor of "earning one's cape" takes on weighty significance when viewed through the lens of developmental theory. As a licensed psychotherapist, I often discuss with my clients how, by the age of seven, individuals are at a crucial juncture in their development. At this point, their thoughts, memories, and belief systems start to solidify, and they begin to internalize the messages and expectations presented to them by society and their immediate surroundings. Thus, **the metaphorical cape, then, becomes symbolic of the inner beliefs and perceptions that individuals have absorbed during this formative period. It is not merely an external symbol of societal expectations but a living manifestation of one's self-concept, self-worth, and understanding of their place in the world.** This emblematic cape encapsulates the beliefs women have internalized about their capabilities, their inherent worth, and the roles they believe they should fulfill.

By blending the concept of developmental theory with the metaphor of "earning one's cape," we show how the experiences and expectations of early life greatly influence the developmental journey. I want to recognize that the cape's fabric is intricately woven with the threads of these experiences, embedding them deeply in an individual's psyche. In essence, "earning your cape" serves as a profound exploration of the intersection between developmental theory and personal identity. It highlights how early experiences, shaped by one's biopsychosocial development, are intimately interwoven into the very essence of one's metaphorical cape, ultimately influencing the trajectory of self-discovery and the realization of one's unique strengths and potential.

Family Dynamics and Early Role Modeling

In the complicated mosaic of a young girl's life, family dynamics emerge as intense architects, playing a pivotal role in shaping her foundational understanding of womanhood. The roles enacted by her mother, father, siblings, and extended family members provide her with living models of what it means to be a woman. These observations, often communicated through unspoken cues and behaviors, construct a fundamental blueprint that molds the expectations and responsibilities she may later feel compelled to fulfill.

One moving story that exemplifies this dynamic is that of Amelia, who grew up in a household where her mother assumed the role of the primary caregiver, tending to the needs of the family, while her father took on the role of the breadwinner. Amelia admired her mother's nurturing qualities and recognized the importance of her contributions, but she also witnessed the strain and sacrifices it imposed on her mother's life. Amelia's parents never explicitly articulated that she should follow in her mother's footsteps. Instead, the messages were conveyed through subtleties, unspoken expectations, and the roles modeled within the family structure. As Amelia transitioned into adolescence and adulthood, she found herself navigating a complex inner conflict. On one hand, she aspired to pursue a demanding career that aligned with her personal aspirations and potential. On the other hand, she struggled with the unspoken expectation, deeply ingrained by years of observation, that she should prioritize family and caregiving.

Ultimately, "family dynamics and early role modeling" serves as a thought-provoking exploration of the intersection between family systems and personal identity. It emphasizes the importance of self-awareness and the ability to critically examine the roles and expectations inherited from early life within the family system. By doing so, individuals can chart a path toward self-discovery that is grounded in authenticity and empowerment, rather than conformity to preconceived notions of womanhood influenced by family systems.

Societal Messages and Cultural Norms

Beyond the family unit, society at large exerts a significant influence, often subtly dictating what is considered "appropriate" for women. These societal messages are pervasive, permeating various facets of life, including media representations, educational systems, and cultural traditions. From a young age, girls are exposed to stereotypical portrayals of women in television, movies, and books, which frequently reinforce traditional roles like the nurturing mother or the self-sacrificing wife. The impact of societal messages becomes especially pronounced when examined through the lens of personal decision-making and identity formation. These messages serve as a continuous undercurrent that shapes women's perceptions of themselves and the roles they believe they should fulfill. They extend beyond mere stereotypes and often manifest as unspoken expectations that influence how you perceive your potential and the choices available to you.

Educational settings, for instance, can inadvertently limit a girl's perception of her potential by subtly steering her toward certain paths and discouraging traits or pursuits deemed "unfeminine." This can manifest in the classroom when girls are subtly guided away from STEM (science, technology, engineering, and mathematics) fields or discouraged from pursuing leadership roles. Such pressures to conform to preconceived roles can result in a gradual loss of individuality and an ongoing sense of being trapped within a predefined narrative. Additionally, the impact of societal expectations is further compounded by the influence of individuals who hold significance in one's life, such as parents, teachers, mentors, and peers. These influential figures often reflect and reinforce the broader societal norms and expectations. They may offer guidance based on these entrenched beliefs, even when they believe they are acting in the individual's best interest. In this complex web of influence, you can find yourself contending with a dual pressure—societal expectations that inhabit the world around you and the well-intentioned guidance from influential figures who may inadvertently perpetuate these expectations.

Internalization and Self-Perception

As external influences from society, family, and influential figures permeate a young girl's life, they gradually become internalized, significantly shaping how she sees herself and her role within the world. This internalization process is a central focus of counseling theories that seek to understand how individuals develop their self-concept and navigate the complexities of identity formation.

Albert Bandura emerged from humble beginnings to become a driving force in understanding human behavior. Growing up in a small Canadian town, he was fascinated by the complexities of human nature from an early age. Bandura's groundbreaking research on social cognitive theory, which emphasized the role of observational learning and self-efficacy in shaping behavior, revolutionized our understanding of how individuals acquire new skills and attitudes.

Bandura's social cognitive theory resonates strongly with understanding self-perception. Bandura suggests that individuals learn through observation, imitation, and modeling, with self-efficacy—a person's belief in their ability to achieve specific goals—playing a pivotal role in shaping behavior. The internalization of societal and familial expectations can be viewed through the lens of social learning. Young girls observe the roles and behaviors of women around them and internalize these observed norms, which subsequently influence their self-efficacy and self-perception.

Going back to Erik Erikson's psychosocial theory of development, individuals undergo a series of psychosocial crises throughout their lives, each of which centers on a fundamental conflict. In the context of the development process, the conflict of "identity versus role confusion" is particularly pertinent. Adolescents and young adults deal with questions of self-identity and the roles they should assume in society. The internalization of external expectations can exacerbate this conflict, potentially leading to role confusion as young girls strive to reconcile their authentic selves with the roles they believe they should fulfill.

The metaphorical cape, growing heavier with each added expectation, aligns with the concept of psychological burdens described in transactional analysis (TA) theory. Eric Berne, a Canadian-born psychiatrist and psychoanalyst, reshaped the landscape of psychology with his groundbreaking theory of TA. Through his insightful exploration of human interactions, Berne sought to demystify the intricacies of relationships and communication. His seminal work, "Games People Play," catapulted TA into the mainstream, offering practical insights into understanding and improving interpersonal dynamics. Berne's legacy continues to influence fields ranging from therapy to organizational behavior, underscoring the enduring relevance of his contributions to the understanding of human behavior.

Eric Berne stated that individuals carry "scripts" or life accounts shaped by early experiences and external influences. These scripts can become limiting and weigh individuals down, impeding personal growth and self-actualization. The internalization of societal and familial expectations can contribute to the development of such scripts, which may hinder self-esteem, career choices, relationships, and overall well-being. The challenge faced by many women, as discussed here, aligns with the importance of congruence between one's self-concept and one's actual experience. The journey to untangle ingrained beliefs and redefine one's figurative cape to align with aspirations and values closely parallels the therapeutic process of self-discovery and personal growth.

In essence, "internalization and self-perception" offers a thoughtful exploration of the internalization of external influences and its impact on self-esteem, choices, and overall prosperity. By incorporating past experiences, and integrating counseling theories, we validate the complexity of the internalization process and the transformative potential of untangling deeply ingrained beliefs. My goal is to take you on a liberating journey of rediscovering your authentic selves, unburdened by the weight of societal and familial expectations.

Cultural Influences and Their Lasting Impressions

It is important to me that you understand that the metaphorical "capes" you wear begins with an examination of the intricate cultural landscapes you navigate. Culture serves as the fertile soil in which the seeds of beliefs are sown and nurtured. It is within this cultural context that societal expectations, gender roles, and ideals of femininity take root and grow. I feel compelled to draw inspiration from various counseling theories and concepts that display the intricate interplay between culture, identity, and societal norms. Culture represents a critical part of the macrosystem that shapes a woman's perception of her role within society. The deeply embedded traditional gender roles and expectations found in many societies are a testament to the pervasive influence of culture on personal identity.

The metaphor of "capes" worn by women is symbolic of these cultural expectations. For generations, culture has often prescribed specific roles for women, emphasizing traits such as nurturing, compliance, and beauty as ideals of femininity. These expectations can be particularly restrictive, defining a narrow pathway for women to follow. However, it is essential to recognize that culture is not static; it evolves over time. There is a gradual but significant shift in many cultures toward more diverse and empowering representations of womanhood. This shift celebrates women for their strength, intelligence, independence, and resilience. It is a testament to the power of societal evolution and the capacity to challenge deeply ingrained norms. As culture undergoes this transformation, it permits the redefining of the representational "cape." What was once a symbol of confinement and limitation is being transformed into a powerful symbol of liberation. The evolving cultural landscape allows you to explore and redefine your identities beyond traditional roles and expectations. It empowers you to question and challenge the "cape" you've been handed and to design one that aligns with your aspirations, values, and authentic self.

The Power of Media in Shaping Beliefs

The influence of television and movies in shaping our beliefs and perceptions cannot be overstated. Media representations, particularly those of women, have long been a subject of intense scrutiny within the fields of psychology and media studies. Let's consider the influence of media through the lens of social cognitive theory. This theory, previously discussed by Albert Bandura, highlights the role of observational learning and modeling in shaping behavior and beliefs. In the context of media, individuals, especially young girls, often observe and internalize the behaviors, roles, and values portrayed by characters onscreen. This process can significantly influence their self-concept and perceptions of societal roles. Moreover, media plays a pivotal role in constructing social reality. Historically, the media has frequently depicted women in relation to men, portraying them as secondary characters or mere supporters of male protagonists. This skewed representation reinforces the notion that women's stories are secondary, a narrative backdrop to the central male experience. Such portrayals contribute to the internalization of gender roles and expectations, further influencing how girls perceive their potential and place in society.

I cannot talk about the media without discussing the work of Alison Bechdel, an American cartoonist, writer, and memoirist. She is renowned for her insightful exploration of identity, family dynamics, and LGBTQ+ themes in her graphic novels. Through her compelling storytelling and distinctive artistic style, Bechdel has captivated readers with narratives that challenge societal norms and offer profound reflections on the human experience. The Bechdel test is a simple measure for assessing gender representation in films. It evaluates whether a work of fiction features at least two women who talk to each other about something other than a man.

Many films and TV shows historically have failed this test, as they often lack meaningful interactions between female characters that are unrelated to male characters or romantic interests. This deficiency reinforces the idea that women's experiences are primarily defined by their relationships with men, diminishing their individual agency and identity. However, the media landscape is evolving, offering a glimmer of hope. The surge of female-led accounts and the emergence of complex, independent female characters are a testament to this change. These portrayals challenge the traditional "cape," offering new patterns and designs that showcase women as the protagonists of their own stories. They present women as individuals with their narratives, aspirations, and struggles, rather than relegating them to supporting roles in someone else's script.

Societal Norms and the Glass Ceiling

In the grand theater of society, roles and expectations are often scripted for individuals based on their gender, and women have long been handed a predefined set of lines and actions to follow. Central to this narrative is the concept of the "glass ceiling," a symbolic and pervasive metaphor representing the often unspoken, yet highly tangible, barrier that impedes women from ascending to the upper echelons of the corporate world. As we examine the concept of the glass ceiling, it is crucial to consider the interconnected inequities faced by women, including unequal pay, underrepresentation in C-suite positions, and their broader societal implications.

Unequal Pay: The issue of unequal pay, often referred to as the gender pay gap, is a glaring manifestation of the glass ceiling's impact. Women, despite qualifications, experience, and dedication, continue to earn less than their male counterparts. Drawing insights from pay equity theory, pay equity theory, created by Esther Peterson who served to improve labor standards and was an advocate for women's rights, which put forward the notion that individuals should receive equal pay for equal work, we recognize the injustice embedded within this systemic problem. This unequal compensation not only limits your financial independence but also reinforces the message that your contributions are undervalued. Addressing this issue is not only a matter of economic justice but also a critical step toward breaking the glass ceiling.

Underrepresentation in C-Suite Positions: Another facet of the glass ceiling's influence is the stark underrepresentation of women in C-suite executive positions. The scarcity of women in top leadership roles, often attributed to gender bias and discriminatory practices, highlights the structural impediments women face in professional journeys. By drawing parallels to theories of organizational behavior, we can discern how these biases perpetuate workplace inequalities. The glass ceiling's presence in the upper tiers of organizations sends a powerful message about the perceived limits of women's leadership capabilities.

Societal Inequality as a Whole: Beyond the workplace, the concept of the glass ceiling extends to the broader societal context. It underscores how deeply ingrained gender norms and expectations can restrict women's progress in all spheres of life. This includes political representation, educational attainment, and access to resources and opportunities.

Advocacy for Change: The silver lining in this narrative is the growing awareness and acknowledgment of these barriers. Women and allies are increasingly advocating for gender equality and the dismantling of the glass ceiling. Initiatives aimed at shattering this metaphorical barrier are gaining momentum. These efforts are underpinned by a collective realization that when women thrive and are afforded equal opportunities, societies as a whole prosper. By dismantling the glass ceiling, we not only create a fairer and more just professional landscape but also pave the way for broader societal transformations, where the potential and contributions of all individuals are valued and celebrated.

Redefining the Cape: A Collective Endeavor

As we continue to explore the uniqueness of our capes, we realize that these garments are not just personal but collective. The threads are spun from shared experiences, societal narratives, and cultural norms. These capes have been woven over generations, handed down through time, shaping the experiences and aspirations of countless women. However, just as these capes have been woven over time, they can also be unraveled and rewoven to better reflect the evolving identities and ambitions of women in today's world.

The Collective Nature of Capes: The capes that you wear are not isolated garments but interconnected threads in the fabric of society. They are woven together through shared experiences, common struggles, and the societal narratives that define womanhood. This collective aspect highlights the need for a collective endeavor in redefining these capes.

Honoring the Past while Embracing the Future: It's essential to emphasize that breaking free from traditional narratives doesn't necessitate discarding our past but rather reinterpreting it to suit our present and future. Redefining the cape is a process that demands intention. It's about finding space between honoring our heritage and embracing our individuality, respecting tradition, and challenging the status quo. We must acknowledge the wisdom of the past while forging a path toward a more inclusive and equitable future.

Chapter 2: Breaking Free from Expectations
Reflective Questions

1. What are the most significant expectations you've imposed on yourself, or others have imposed on you?

2. How have these expectations affected your well-being and relationships?

3. What values and aspirations drive your desire to break free from these expectations?

4. What theories resonated with you and why?

5. In what areas of your life do you find it most challenging to break free from societal expectations?

Exercise 1: Compose a letter to yourself, listing the expectations you are ready to let go of and explaining why they no longer serve you.

Exercise 2: Identify one concrete action you can take to challenge an expectation that has been weighing you down. Implement this action and journal about the experience.

"Don't think about making women fit the world—think about making the world fit women."
– Gloria Steinem

CHAPTER 3

THE SUCCESS OF THE CAPE

As the sun dipped low on the horizon, casting a golden hue over the quaint coastal town of Harborview, Meagan stood atop the rugged cliffs, her cape billowing in the salty breeze. From afar, she appeared the epitome of success—a thriving career, a picturesque seaside home, and a confident stride that commanded attention. To the world, Meagan was the embodiment of achievement, a beacon of inspiration for aspiring women everywhere.

Yet, beneath the smokescreen of accomplishment, Meagan harbored a secret turmoil that only the crashing waves bore witness to. For years, she had chased after society's definition of success, climbing the corporate ladder with unwavering determination and sacrificing pieces of herself along the way.

At first, the accolades and promotions were intoxicating, validating her worth in the eyes of her peers and superiors. But as time passed, the pressure to maintain her façade became suffocating, like the continuous tide eroding away at the sturdy cliffs below her feet.

With each passing day, Meagan found herself caught in a relentless cycle of striving for perfection, juggling the demands of her career with the expectations placed upon her as a woman in a male-dominated industry. She wore her cape of success like armor, shielding herself from the vulnerabilities that lurked beneath the surface.

But behind closed doors, the cracks began to show. The late nights at the office took a toll on her relationships, leaving her feeling isolated and disconnected from those she loved. The constant pressure to excel left her exhausted and drained, her once vibrant spirit dimmed by the weight of expectations.

As Meagan gazed out at the vast expanse of the ocean stretching before her, she couldn't help but feel a longing for something more. Success, it seemed, was a double-edged sword, promising fulfillment yet causing a heavy toll in return.

In that moment of quiet contemplation, Meagan realized that true success wasn't measured by external accolades or societal expectations. It wasn't about climbing to the top at any cost, but rather finding fulfillment in both her personal and professional life.

With a newfound sense of clarity, Meagan made a silent vow to herself to redefine success on her own terms, to embrace her vulnerabilities, and to prioritize her own well-being above all else. As the sun dipped below the horizon, casting the sky ablaze with hues of pink and orange, Meagan felt a glimmer of hope ignite within her. For in that moment she understood that true success wasn't about reaching the summit, but rather embarking on the journey with authenticity and purpose, cape fluttering in the wind as she forged her own path forward.

Women deal with multifaceted pressures as they strive for excellence within various roles. These pressures, shaped by societal expectations and internalized beliefs, create a challenging landscape that affects women both personally and professionally. Let's explore the consequences of this relentless pursuit of perfection and the difficulty you often encounter when trying to set boundaries and prioritize self-care.

The Myth of the Superwoman

The myth of the superwoman not only looms large but often transforms into a proverbial truth in the lives of countless women. It dictates that you should not just excel but effortlessly excel in every facet of life. Society's portrayals reinforce this myth, presenting you as capable of seamlessly balancing high-powered careers, nurturing motherhood, fulfilling partnerships, and active community involvement. Furthermore, it suggests that you should perform these roles without displaying any signs of struggle, vulnerability, or imperfection. This societal pressure runs so deep that it becomes an internalized truth. It's as if the myth of the superwoman takes root within your self-perception, shaping your beliefs about what you should achieve and how you should navigate life's complexities. To illustrate the extreme impact of this internalized myth, we turn to the story of Leslie, a brilliant scientist and mother of two.

On the surface, Leslie appeared to have it all: a successful career, a loving family, and active participation in community projects. However, behind closed doors, Leslie danced with the relentless pursuit of perfection. This unyielding quest wasn't just an external expectation; it had become a part of Leslie's own narrative, an unspoken truth she felt compelled to uphold.

Leslie's story serves as a poignant example of how the myth of the superwoman becomes more than a societal expectation; it becomes a personal truth that one carries. In her tireless efforts to meet the ever-expanding expectations of herself and those around her, she found herself caught in a perpetual cycle of striving, often at the cost of her own well-being. Leslie's experience underscores the immense pressure you may encounter in your own daily life, a pressure that can lead to burnout, mental health challenges, and strained relationships.

The Unrealistic Expectation of Perfection

The perpetuation of the superwoman myth is the result of a complex interplay between external, internal, and organizational influences. Understanding these factors from an organizational perspective adds another layer of insight into the challenges you may face. Externally, society plays a significant role in reinforcing these unrealistic expectations. Media portrayals, cultural norms, and societal pressures bombard women with images and narratives that suggest they should effortlessly manage high-powered careers, maintain picture-perfect family lives, and excel in various social and community roles. These societal pressures are not isolated but are often mirrored and exacerbated within organizational cultures.

Organizations, consciously or unconsciously, contribute to these external pressures. Workplace cultures can perpetuate the superwoman myth by promoting overwork, unrealistic productivity expectations, and an absence of work-life balance. The demand for constant availability and dedication can leave women feeling compelled to fulfill both their professional roles and societal roles simultaneously. Internally, women often possess an innate drive to excel, viewing their accomplishments as a reflection of their self-worth. This internalized belief can fuel the pursuit of perfection, and organizations may inadvertently reinforce this drive through reward structures that prioritize long hours and achievement at any cost. From an organizational perspective, the implications of these factors are significant. Burnout, high turnover rates among female employees, and a lack of diversity in leadership roles can be traced back to these unrealistic expectations. Moreover, organizations that fail to address these issues may suffer from decreased employee morale, lower productivity, and difficulty in attracting and retaining top talent.

To address these challenges, organizations should prioritize creating inclusive and supportive cultures. This may involve reevaluating reward systems, promoting work-life balance, and providing resources and support for employees to manage stress and perfectionist tendencies. By acknowledging and addressing these organizational aspects, companies can contribute to a more equitable and healthy work environment for women, ultimately benefiting both women and the organization as a whole.

The Consequences of Relentless Pursuit

The relentless pursuit of the superwoman ideal is not merely a passing phase but a lifelong journey. Statistics and research shed light on the extent to which individuals spend the majority of their lives navigating these challenges:

1. Work-Life Balance Struggles: Studies have shown that approximately 66% of women report facing difficulties in achieving a satisfactory work-life balance throughout their careers (*Source: Pew Research Center*). This struggle often persists from early adulthood into middle age and beyond.

2. Mental Health Challenges: According to the World Health Organization (WHO), depression is currently the leading cause of disability among women, and women are more likely than men to experience depression during their lifetime (*Source: WHO*). According to the Anxiety and Depression Association of America (ADAA), approximately 33% of women will experience an anxiety disorder at some point in their lifetime, compared to about 22% of men.

3. Impact on Relationships: A comprehensive study by the American Psychological Association (APA) highlights that individuals who face persistent work-related stress and wrestle with work-life balance report higher levels of conflict in their relationships, including marital dissatisfaction and disrupted family dynamics (*Source: APA*).

4. Burnout Prevalence: A survey conducted by Gallup found that approximately 23% of full-time employees report feeling burned out often or always (*Source: Gallup*). Among working mothers, the prevalence of burnout due to the juggling act of multiple roles is notably higher.

5. Career Advancement Challenges: The gender pay gap, which is a reflection of unequal opportunities and compensation for women, remains a pervasive issue. According to the U.S. Bureau of Labor Statistics, women earn, on average, only 82 cents for every dollar earned by men (*Source: U.S. Bureau of Labor Statistics*). This wage gap persists throughout women's careers and significantly impacts their financial well-being.

The relentless pursuit of the superwoman ideal definitely imposes lasting consequences on your life. These interconnected challenges illustrate why many of you find it difficult to "take the cape off," as societal expectations and structural barriers perpetuate the pressure to strive for perfection and endure this superwoman role.

Chapter 3: The Courage to Say No
Reflective Questions

1. Discuss a time when saying "yes" to commitments that didn't align with your values led to stress or burnout.

2. What fears or concerns have held you back from setting boundaries and saying "no"?

3. How would your life change if you became more assertive in setting boundaries?

4. Are there specific situations or relationships where you find it especially challenging to say "no"?

5. Have you had symptoms of burnout, stress, or depression? What can you or did you do to improve your situation?

Exercise 1: Practice assertiveness by setting boundaries in a specific area of your life. Write about the experience and any challenges you faced.

Exercise 2: Create a list of your top priorities and values. Use this list as a reference when deciding whether to say "yes" or "no" to new commitments.

"The things that make us different, those are our superpowers."
– Lena Waithe

CHAPTER 4

WHY CAN'T YOU TAKE THE CAPE OFF?

After a particularly grueling day, Bella steps out of a seemingly never-ending meeting. The discussions were intense, requiring her to navigate complex issues while managing a diverse array of opinions. Exiting the boardroom, she feels the cumulative weight of the day's challenges bearing down on her. Her day was filled with back-to-back commitments: tight project deadlines, sudden problems needing her immediate attention, and a constant barrage of demands for her input and expertise. Feeling utterly depleted, Bella dials her friend Marianne. The moment Marianne picks up, Bella's composure unravels. Tears she's been suppressing all day surge forth as she confides in Marianne, her voice trembling with the strain of her emotions.

"I just can't seem to catch a break," Bella divulges, sharing the ordeal of her day—not just the exhausting meeting but the constant decision-making, the unreasonable expectations, and the incessant need to excel. She recounts how her lunch was a sandwich eaten hastily at her desk, accompanied by a relentless influx of emails, each marked as urgent. Marianne listens intently as Bella reveals the range of her responsibilities. At work, she's the cornerstone of her team, constantly pushing for excellence and spearheading initiatives. At home, her role is equally demanding, where she's the central figure in her family's life, managing schedules, assisting with homework, and upkeeping the home. Personal dreams, like pursuing a painting class or joining a book club, remain on the back burner, overshadowed by her commitments to her family and career.

During this conversation with Marianne, Bella admits to feeling entrapped by a cycle of expectations and responsibilities. She shares a poignant realization: despite feeling crushed under the weight, she sees no viable way to lighten her load. The mere thought of not fulfilling her own or others' expectations fills her with anxiety. "It's as if I'm chained to this cape," she expresses, "and the idea of removing it leaves me frozen with fear, scared of letting everyone down."

Marianne suggests that Bella might look for areas in her life to pare down or delegate, but Bella lays out the stark reality of her circumstances. Each task appears critical, each duty indispensable. She conveys a sense of acknowledgment, recognizing the burden of the cape yet feeling obligated to wear it, convinced there's no other way forward at this moment.

Their dialogue is a candid revelation of Bella's inner world. It's a moment where the façade of the always capable and resilient woman fractures, exposing the deep fatigue and longing for a change hidden beneath. Yet, despite this moment of candid vulnerability, Bella remains tied to her current life rhythm, unsure of how to begin the transformation she so earnestly desires. Bella realizes that she cannot remove the cape.

The challenge of shedding the cape is a complex and deeply rooted issue that women face throughout life. Several interrelated factors contribute to the enduring challenge of taking off the cape:

1. Internalized Beliefs: You often internalize societal expectations that you should be selfless caregivers and high-achieving professionals simultaneously. These deeply ingrained beliefs lead you to prioritize the needs of others over your own. The prospect of self-care can be accompanied by feelings of guilt and self-criticism. Based on what you believe dictates how your actions appear in the world. If you believe you have to help others and take on responsibilities despite what you may need, then you have a tendency to do so while eventually feeling the burden you carry.

2. Fear of Judgment: The fear of judgment creates a psychological barrier to setting healthy boundaries and asserting one's need for self-care. Women, in your roles as professionals, caregivers, partners, and friends, you often find yourself in a perpetual state of overextension. The thought of saying "no" or stepping back, even slightly, to tend to your well-being is accompanied by a cascade of worrisome thoughts: *What will people think? Will they see me as selfish? Incompetent? Will my colleagues doubt my commitment? Will my family think I don't care?*

These questions are not trivial. They stem from a deeply ingrained societal narrative that equates a woman's worth with her selflessness and her ability to juggle multiple responsibilities seamlessly. This narrative perpetuates the myth of the superwoman—the invincible female figure who can handle any challenge thrown her way without breaking a sweat. The pressure to uphold this pretense of invincibility can indeed be paralyzing as it leaves little room for vulnerability, rest, and the acknowledgment that one is human, with limits. The fear of judgment can lead to a cycle of silence and isolation. You may feel that the struggles are unique to you—that you are the only one failing to live up to these unrealistic standards. This isolation can prevent you from seeking support, sharing your experiences, or finding solace in the shared struggles of others. The irony is that while many women fear judgment for not being able to do it all, they often realize that they are far from alone in their feelings of being overwhelmed and under-supported.

Addressing the fear of judgment requires a multifaceted approach. It begins with fostering self-awareness and challenging the internalized narratives that dictate that a woman's worth is measured by her productivity and capacity for self-sacrifice. It is important to understand that the fear of judgment is a shared one, and that strength lies in vulnerability and the collective rejection of impossible standards set forth for all women.

Societal attitudes and expectations need to shift to value self-care and well-being as essential components of success, rather than as signs of weakness or self-indulgence. This cultural shift can start small, within families, workplaces, and communities, as you challenge the stigma associated with setting boundaries and prioritizing self-care. In essence, the fear of judgment is a formidable obstacle to achieving balance and wellness, but it is not insurmountable. Through introspection and societal change, the cycle of fear and overextension can be broken, paving the way for a more compassionate and realistic understanding of what it means to be truly strong.

3. Lack of Support: You could lack a robust support system that would enable you to share the burden of responsibilities. The absence of equitable sharing of caregiving and household duties can compound the challenges of wearing the cape. The weight is often felt daily with the significant challenges you face when you do not have a robust support system to help distribute the myriad responsibilities you carry. This lack of support is particularly pronounced when it comes to the equitable sharing of caregiving and household duties, a reality that many women navigate daily.

Let's discuss Kennedy's story. Kennedy is seen as a pillar of strength in her community and workplace. She's the person others turn to for guidance, support, and leadership. At work, she's admired for her ability to lead teams and manage projects with a calm and decisive demeanor. In her personal life, she's the rock for her family and friends, always ready to lend an ear or a hand. However, Kennedy's role as a leader and a go-to person comes with its own set of challenges. Despite being surrounded by people who respect and look up to her, she finds herself in a paradoxical state of isolation when it comes to receiving support. Her colleagues and loved ones often assume that because she is so capable and strong, she doesn't need help or that her resources for managing stress and challenges are limitless.

This perception leaves Kennedy without a confidante to turn to when she faces her own struggles. The narrative explores a particularly trying period in Kennedy's life when the pressures of her professional responsibilities, combined with personal trials, bring her to a brink. She feels the acute absence of a support system where she can be vulnerable, share her burdens, and seek guidance. Kennedy's story reaches a critical point one evening after a long day of back-to-back meetings and resolving family issues, where she sits in her car, overwhelmed by a sense of solitude and exhaustion. It's a moment of introspection where she confronts the reality of her situation—being the support pillar for everyone else has left her without a pillar of her own to lean on. Kennedy sits in her car for over an hour trying to figure out a new plan, but she eventually hops out of the car without any resolution, telling herself there must be another way.

Through Kennedy's experience, we should realize the importance of recognizing the needs of those who are typically seen as strong and independent. We must become advocates for creating environments, both in the workplace and in personal spheres, where even the most resilient individuals feel comfortable expressing their vulnerabilities and seeking help is the norm. This overview highlights the popularized term of "checking on your strong friends." It is imperative that we provide mutual support and understanding, ensuring that no one, not even the seemingly strongest among us, have to bear their burdens alone.

4. Cultural and Societal Expectations: Societal emphasis on productivity and achievement can create the perception that slowing down or taking a break is unacceptable. You may feel compelled to keep pushing forward, regardless of the toll it takes on your well-being. This societal emphasis can create a pervasive perception that taking a moment to breathe, to slow down, or to indulge in a well-deserved break is not just frowned upon but is fundamentally unacceptable. You may find yourself caught in a cycle of striving and accomplishing, driven by a fear that pausing—even momentarily—could be construed as a lack of dedication or ambition. This societal narrative is not confined to the professional realm but extends into every facet of life. In the workplace, this can translate into a culture where long hours are glorified, and time off is seen as a luxury or, worse, a sign of a lack of commitment. You could feel an acute pressure to prove yourself in environments that equate constant availability with competence and dedication. The expectation to be perpetually engaged and productive can lead to a work culture where the lines between personal and professional life blur, further exacerbating the challenge of finding balance.

At home, the pressures can be just as intense. Societal and cultural norms often uphold the ideal of the selfless woman who prioritizes the needs and well-being of her family above her own. This expectation can make it difficult for you to justify time spent on self-care or personal interests, as such activities can be perceived as selfish or indulgent. The relentless push to nurture, care, and provide can leave little room for individual pursuits or even basic rest, reinforcing the notion that your value is tied to your ability to juggle multiple roles seamlessly.

The toll of these expectations on well-being cannot be overstated. The constant drive to meet and exceed these societal standards can lead to burnout, stress, and a host of physical and mental health issues. Yet, the fear of stepping back, of being perceived as not doing enough, can be paralyzing, trapping individuals in a cycle of continuous exertion that disregards the essential human need for rest and rejuvenation.

In recognizing these challenges, it becomes clear that there is a profound need for a cultural shift—a reevaluation of the values that prioritize achievement over well-being. Such a shift would encourage a more balanced approach to life, where productivity is not the sole metric of success, and where taking time for yourself is not only accepted but celebrated as a necessary component of a healthy, fulfilling life.

Strategies for Acknowledging and Addressing the Pressures

While the challenges are significant, here are some comprehensive strategies for you to acknowledge and address the tough pressures you face:

1. Recognizing the Myth: In the journey toward wellness and balance, the pivotal first step is dismantling the pervasive myth of the superwoman—a societal archetype that compels women to strive for an unattainable standard of perfection across all areas of your lives. Recognizing this myth for what it truly is—an unrealistic and harmful construct that we all unconsciously abide by—is essential in reclaiming your well-being and mitigating the risk of burnout and emotional exhaustion.

Let's meet Harper. She is a dedicated environmental lawyer and a mother of two who embodies the struggle against the superwoman myth. Her days are a marathon of court preparations, client meetings, household management, and attentive parenting. Despite her accomplishments, Harper grapples with a persistent sense of inadequacy, driven by the feeling that she must excel in every facet of her life to validate her worth.

The turning point for Harper comes during an unexpected quiet moment on a late Sunday evening. After the children are asleep and the house is silent, Harper stumbles upon an article discussing the superwoman myth. The article outlines the unrealistic expectations placed on women to perform flawlessly in their careers, while also being perfect caregivers, partners, and friends. It's a revelatory moment for Harper. She sees her own struggles reflected in the words and realizes that the incessant pressure she's been putting on herself is a manifestation of a broader societal issue, not a personal failing.

This realization sparks a profound shift in Harper's perspective. She begins to see the unrealistic standards she's been striving to meet not as benchmarks of success but as shackles that have been limiting her sense of self and well-being. The article serves as a mirror, reflecting back to her the unsustainable nature of the superwoman ideal and the toll it has taken on her mental and emotional health. Armed with this new understanding, Harper starts to challenge the superwoman myth in her daily life. She initiates open conversations with her colleagues and friends about the pressures of trying to "do it all" and discovers that her experiences are far from unique. These discussions foster a sense of solidarity and mutual support, providing Harper and her circle with a shared vocabulary to articulate their struggles and aspirations for a more balanced life. Harper takes concrete steps to adjust her own expectations of herself. She begins to prioritize her tasks, identifying what truly needs her attention and what can be delegated or postponed. She starts setting aside time for activities that replenish her energy and bring her joy, such as reading, yoga, and nature walks with her children.

Through Harper's journey, we see the transformative power of recognizing the superwoman myth. It showcases how breaking free from the grip of unrealistic expectations can open the door to a more fulfilling, balanced, and sustainable way of living. Harper's story becomes a beacon of hope and a guide for others navigating similar paths, underscoring the importance of awareness, self-reflection, and community in overcoming the pressures of modern womanhood.

2. Self-Compassion: In the journey toward wellness and personal fulfillment, self-compassion emerges as a critical strategy. It's about extending to oneself the same kindness, care, and understanding one would offer to a good friend. This approach challenges the often harsh and critical inner voice you may harbor, encouraging a nurturing and forgiving attitude toward yourself.

Aubry, as a seasoned school principal and mother of three, epitomizes the challenge of practicing self-compassion in a high-stress, high-expectation environment. Her days are a blend of administrative duties, educational leadership, parenting, and community involvement. She holds herself to exceedingly high standards, often critiquing her performance in every role she plays.

One evening, after a particularly challenging day at the school followed by a hectic evening at home, Aubry finds herself overwhelmed by feelings of inadequacy. She had dealt with a difficult situation at school that didn't resolve as she had hoped, and at home, she felt disconnected from her children, unable to provide them with the attention she felt they deserved.

It's during this moment of vulnerability that Aubry stumbles upon a self-help book (about self-compassion) left on her nightstand, a gift she had received but never opened. Curiosity piqued, she begins to read and is immediately drawn into the concept of treating oneself with kindness, grace, and understanding.

Inspired by what she reads, Aubry embarks on a journey to cultivate self-compassion. She starts a daily practice of reflecting on her experiences, identifying moments where her inner critic is particularly harsh, and consciously replacing those thoughts with more compassionate and supportive messages. She learns to acknowledge her efforts and intentions, even when the outcomes are not as she expected. She also starts to treat her perceived shortcomings with understanding rather than judgment.

Aubry also adopts the practice of mindfulness which helps her become more aware of her critical inner voice and offers her strategies to counteract it with compassion. She sets aside time each week for activities that nurture her well-being, such as meditation, journaling, and walks in nature, recognizing these moments as essential for her mental and emotional health.

Over time, Aubry notices a shift in how she responds to challenges both at work and home. She becomes more forgiving of herself, more resilient in the face of setbacks, and more present and engaged with her children. Her relationships with her colleagues and family deepen, reflecting the positive changes in her self-dialogue and attitude.

Through Aubry's story, the transformative act of self-compassion being developed creates a positive impact on an individual's mental, emotional, and relational well-being. It illustrates how adopting a kinder, more understanding approach to your life can lead to greater resilience, satisfaction, and a joyful life. Aubry's journey serves as an inspiring example of how self-compassion can be a powerful antidote to the pressures and challenges of modern life.

3. Setting Boundaries: The act of setting boundaries is a critical skill in managing the complexities of modern life. It involves understanding and communicating your limits in both personal and professional contexts. By learning to say no and delegating tasks, you can protect your time, energy, and well-being, preventing the overextension that leads to burnout.

Bonnie, a talented software developer and a devoted mother of twins, faces the daily challenge of balancing a demanding career with her family life. Known in her workplace for her problem-solving skills and dedication, Bonnie often finds herself inundated with requests for help on projects, even those outside her direct responsibilities. At home, she strives to be an attentive parent, actively participating in her children's education and extracurricular activities.

However, Bonnie's reluctance to set boundaries has left her feeling perpetually drained and struggling to find time for herself and her family. Her desire to meet everyone's expectations at work and at home has become an unsustainable cycle that leaves little space for her personal interests or self-care.

The realization that something needs to change comes one weekend when Bonnie finds herself working on a project deadline while simultaneously trying to manage her children's softball tournament. Overwhelmed and exhausted, she reaches a breaking point where the joy in these activities is overshadowed by stress and fatigue.

This moment of clarity prompts Bonnie to reassess her approach to setting boundaries. She begins by identifying her priorities and limits, acknowledging that she cannot be everything to everyone. At work, Bonnie starts to communicate her capacity more clearly, turning down requests that fall outside her primary responsibilities or when her workload is too high. She also advocates for a more equitable distribution of tasks within her team, highlighting the importance of shared responsibility and support.

At home, Bonnie has open conversations with her family about her need for support and the importance of shared household responsibilities. Together, they create a more balanced approach to chores and activities, allowing Bonnie to carve out time for herself.

Bonnie also learns the power of saying no with kindness and assertiveness, understanding that setting boundaries is not a rejection of others but an act of self-respect, self-care, and a resounding yes to her! She practices delegating tasks, both at work and home, empowering others to contribute and grow while also managing her own workload.

As Bonnie implements these changes, she notices a significant shift in her well-being. She feels more energized, present, and engaged in her activities. Her relationships improve, as does her performance at work, demonstrating the profound impact that setting boundaries can have on various aspects of her life.

Bonnie's story emphasizes how the art of setting boundaries can be challenging, especially in a culture that glorifies busyness and constant availability. We see that the benefits to one's mental, emotional, and physical health can be immense. Bonnie's journey serves as an empowering example of how setting boundaries is a key step in shedding the cape and embracing a fulfilling life.

4. Seeking Support: Building a robust support network is not just beneficial—it's essential for navigating the complexities of life. Having a circle of support can significantly lighten the load of responsibilities, providing both practical help and emotional sustenance during challenging times. This network can include family, friends, colleagues, or community members, each playing a unique role in offering support and encouragement.

Hazel's Scenario

Hazel, an accomplished book editor and single parent, epitomizes the struggle many face in seeking and accepting support. With a demanding career and the responsibilities of raising two young children on her own, Hazel often feels overwhelmed, juggling her professional obligations with her parenting duties. Despite her best efforts, the balancing act is exhausting, and Hazel seldom finds time for herself, which wears on her resilience and well-being.

After a particularly taxing week where work deadlines clashed with her daughter's school play and her son's dental emergency, Hazel realizes that her current approach is unsustainable. The turning point comes when a close friend, noticing Hazel's stress, offers to help with school pickups and meals. Initially, Hazel is reluctant to accept the help, conditioned to believe she should manage everything independently. However, recognizing her fatigue and the genuine offer of support, she decides to accept.

This experience is eye-opening for Hazel. It prompts her to actively seek out and build a stronger support network. She starts by reaching out to other parents in her children's school, forming a carpool group that shares the responsibility of transportation to and from school activities. At work, she opens up to her colleagues about her challenges, finding that many are eager to support her, whether by collaborating more on projects or simply providing a listening ear during tough times.

Hazel also joins a local support group for single parents where she finds a sense of community and understanding. Sharing experiences with others in similar situations provides Hazel with emotional support and practical advice, helping her feel less isolated in her struggles.

As Hazel cultivates these new connections, she notices a profound impact on her life. The shared responsibilities allow her more breathing room in her schedule, reducing her stress and giving her more quality time with her children. Emotionally, the sense of solidarity and understanding from her support network provides a wellspring of strength and comfort.

Hazel's story underscores the importance of actively seeking and accepting support. It illustrates that while independence is valuable, there is immense strength in community and collaboration. Hazel's journey demonstrates that building a support network is a key strategy in managing life's demands, showing that when individuals come together to share burdens and offer assistance, the challenges of life become more manageable and less isolating.

5. Redefining Success: Redefining success on your own terms is a liberating step toward authentic fulfillment. It's about shifting away from society's narrow definitions of achievement and embracing a more holistic view that includes personal well-being, fulfillment, and alignment with your core values and priorities. This perspective acknowledges that striving for perfection is a futile endeavor and recognizes the importance of working toward balance for that moment—that day, in your present space.

Stella, a dedicated non-profit organization director known for her tireless work ethic and commitment to her cause, finds herself at a crossroads. Despite her professional accomplishments and the recognition she receives,

Stella feels an underlying sense of dissatisfaction. She realizes that her definition of success, heavily influenced by societal accolades and professional achievements, has left little room for her personal well-being and the things she values most, like family time, creativity, and community involvement.

The epiphany comes during a rare quiet moment on a weekend retreat, intended as a brief respite from her hectic schedule. Surrounded by nature and detached from her usual routine, Stella reflects on what truly brings her joy and fulfillment. She acknowledges that her relentless pursuit of professional success has come at the cost of her health, relationships, and personal passions.

Motivated by this realization, Stella begins the process of redefining what success means to her. She starts by identifying her core values, such as connection, creativity, and contribution, and then assesses how well her current lifestyle aligns with these values. Stella recognizes that true success for her includes making a meaningful impact through her work but not at the expense of her health or happiness.

She sets new, more holistic goals for herself that encompass various aspects of her life. Professionally, she continues to dedicate herself to her cause but sets clearer boundaries to prevent burnout. She also carves out regular time for creative pursuits, like painting and writing, which reignite her passion and provide a sense of balance. Furthermore, Stella commits to deepening her relationships with family and friends, recognizing these connections as foundational to her happiness and well-being.

As Stella implements these changes, she experiences a profound shift in her sense of fulfillment. She finds that by broadening her definition of success to include personal well-being and alignment with her values, she feels more content, energized, and true to herself. Her relationships flourish, her creativity blossoms, and she feels a renewed sense of purpose in her work.

Through Stella's story, the transformative power of redefining success highlights the importance of introspection, alignment with personal values, and the courage to embrace a more balanced approach to life. Stella's journey serves as an inspiring example of how success, when redefined to encompass holistic well-being, leads to a richer, more satisfying life experience.

These strategies empower you to gradually shed the weight of the cape, reclaim your own well-being, and find a more fulfilling way to navigate the multiple roles you play in your life. The expectation for you to excel in your multiple roles is often seen as virtuous and is glorified as an ideal of femininity. As a result, you grow up internalizing the belief that your worth is intricately tied to your ability to flawlessly balance multiple responsibilities.

Consider Emily, the dedicated teacher who spends her days navigating the complexities of the classroom. For her, and countless women like her, the expectation is to handle these challenges with the grace and efficiency of a superheroine. Women are expected to be composed, always ready to save the day while never faltering in their roles.

However, beneath the surface, many of you secretly grapple with the emotional toll of this relentless pursuit. The weight of societal expectations can be extremely draining, leading to feelings of exhaustion and inadequacy. Emily, for instance, may find herself emotionally drained after a day of supporting her students, and yet she returns home to take on the role of a nurturing in your present space. The pursuit of perfection can become a never-ending marathon where you tirelessly strive to meet unattainable standards. You may find yourself juggling a never-ending to-do list, torn between work deadlines, family needs, and personal aspirations. This constant striving for excellence can leave you mentally exhausted and struggling to find moments of respite.

One of the most dangerous consequences of these unrealistic expectations is the impact on your self-esteem. Society's demands for perfection can erode self-worth, leaving you feeling as though you are never good enough. Sarah from Chapter 1, known as the high-powered executive and mother of two, may often wrestle with feelings of self-doubt, fearing that any display of vulnerability is a failure in the eyes of society. In addition to self-efficacy, impostor syndrome, a psychological pattern where individuals doubt their accomplishments and have a persistent fear of being exposed as a "fraud," often affects women in the workplace. Addressing negative thought patterns and building self-confidence can be crucial in overcoming impostor syndrome.

Example: Lena, a successful marketing manager, constantly feels that she doesn't deserve her position and is afraid others will discover she's not as competent as they believe. Lena learns to challenge and reframe her negative self-perceptions, allowing her to acknowledge her achievements without self-doubt. The toll on a woman's well-being is undeniable. Emotional exhaustion, self-esteem issues, impostor syndrome, and constant juggling of roles can lead to stress, anxiety, and even burnout. It's a silent struggle that many of you may face while simultaneously caught in a cycle of trying to meet the unrelenting demands placed upon you.

Chapter 4: The Art of Self-Care
Reflective Questions

1. How do you currently practice self-care in your life, and how effective is it in nurturing your well-being?
2. Can you identify any barriers or obstacles that prevent you from prioritizing self-care?
3. What self-care activities resonate most with you, and how can you incorporate them into your routine?
4. How can self-care positively impact your physical and emotional health?
5. What role does self-compassion play in your ability to engage in self-care?

Exercise 1: Develop a weekly self-care plan that includes at least three self-care activities. Implement this plan for the next month and journal about your experiences.

Exercise 2: Write a self-compassionate letter to yourself, emphasizing the importance of self-care and self-kindness. Refer to this letter when you need a reminder to prioritize self-care.

"Don't think about making women fit the world—think about making the world fit women."
– Gloria Steinem

CHAPTER 5

THE WEIGHT OF THE CAPE

Felicia's days are a testament to her dedication and efficiency, balancing demanding career responsibilities with family commitments and community service. To the outside world, she is the epitome of success, handling each task with apparent ease. Yet, the façade of invincibility she portrays contradicts the underlying toll of her lifestyle. The intense and unyielding pace at which she operates starts to manifest through various stress-related symptoms, signaling the body's plea for respite.

During an especially taxing week, where professional and personal responsibilities converge, Felicia's resilience is put to the test. She is at the helm of organizing a major conference, orchestrating a community fundraiser, and navigating her teenage son's educational hurdles. Each night, as she tries to find solace in sleep, her mind races with unfinished tasks and looming deadlines, leaving her more exhausted than rejuvenated come morning.

The unrelenting nature of her schedule affords little opportunity for self-care, leading to a noticeable decline in her physical well-being. Persistent headaches, gastrointestinal discomfort, and a persistent backache become her constant companions, yet she presses on, driven by an ingrained belief that her value is tied to her ability to meet and exceed every expectation.

The Short-Term Impact of the Weight of the Cape

The immediate effects of Felicia's sustained efforts to maintain her superwoman status has reached the pinnacle. Stress, exhaustion, and the initial stages of burnout begin to surface, impacting not only her emotional health but also manifesting in physical ailments.

The strategies that you and Felicia can seamlessly integrate into your daily routines to address the anxiety and stress that plague the nights and cloud the days are listed here.

1. Simplified Thought Reframing: Identifying and shifting negative thought patterns to assist in recognizing counterproductive thoughts and gently guiding yourself toward more positive, constructive perspectives.

Basic Stress Reduction Methods: Grounding techniques are a set of strategies designed to "ground" or immediately connect you to the present moment, often used to detract from overwhelming feelings or intense anxiety. They can be particularly effective in managing stress by helping redirect attention away from stressors or negative thought patterns and focusing on the present, which can reduce the intensity of the stress or anxiety being experienced. Here is an overview of how grounding helps reduce stress:

- **Brings Attention to the Present**: Grounding techniques draw attention away from past or future concerns, which are often sources of stress, and focus on the current moment, reducing feelings of overwhelm.

- **Interrupts Negative Thought Patterns**: By shifting focus to the present, grounding techniques can break the cycle of persistent worry or spiraling thoughts that often accompany stress.

- **Activates the Parasympathetic Nervous System**: Engaging in grounding exercises can help stimulate the body's relaxation response (parasympathetic nervous system), reducing the physical symptoms of stress.

- **Enhances Self-awareness**: Regular practice of grounding can increase mindfulness and self-awareness, helping individuals recognize early signs of stress and respond proactively.

Techniques for Grounding

- **5-4-3-2-1 Technique**: This involves identifying and focusing on five things you can see, four things you can touch, three things you can hear, two things you can smell, and one thing you can taste. This technique is effective in bringing your awareness to the present, engaging multiple senses.

- **Deep Breathing**: Concentrate on your breath, taking slow, deep breaths. This helps reduce the "fight or flight" response and promotes a state of calmness.

- **Physical Touch**: Techniques like holding a piece of ice, touching a textured object, or feeling the ground beneath your feet can provide an immediate connection to the present, offering a physical anchor to the now.

- **Mindful Observation**: Choose an object within your sight and focus all your attention on it, noting every detail you can. This can help shift your focus from internal stress to external reality.

- **Progressive Muscle Relaxation**: Tense and then gradually relax different muscle groups in the body. This can reduce physical tension associated with stress and anchor you in the sensation of the present.

- **Visualization**: Imagine a place that makes you feel safe and calm. Engaging all your senses in this visualization can help shift your focus away from stress.

Incorporating these grounding techniques into your daily routine can provide a practical toolset to manage stress effectively, helping maintain a sense of calm and control in the face of life's stressors.

2. Practical Work-Life Balance Tips: Expanding on the concept of work-life balance, it's essential to recognize that achieving a perfect equilibrium between professional and personal life is more of an ongoing process than a static state. **Life's inherent busyness and unforeseeable changes mean that balance is dynamic and can fluctuate day by day or even hour by hour.** The goal is to strive for balance in the moment, acknowledging that what constitutes balance can vary significantly depending on current circumstances and responsibilities. To achieve this, incorporate a daily plan to focus on one specific area and do that very well for the day. Give yourself grace knowing that you may fall short in another arena in your life that day. Each day it is important for you to strive to do well at something instead of falling short in every area within your life.

Setting Realistic Priorities: It's crucial for you and Felicia to identify what's most important, both in your personal and professional lives. This prioritization can change depending on immediate needs and long-term goals. Encouraging you to regularly assess and adjust your priorities helps you focus your time and energy on what truly matters, reducing feelings of being spread too thin.

Establishing Healthy Boundaries: Creating clear boundaries between work and personal life is key to preventing burnout. This might mean setting specific work hours, keeping work communication within those hours, and having dedicated spaces for work and relaxation. However, flexibility is essential; there will be times when work demands more attention and other times when personal life needs to take precedence.

Finding Time for Self-care: Integrating self-care into your routine is vital for maintaining mental, emotional, and physical well-being. Even during busy periods, encouraging small acts of self-care can provide necessary breaks and rejuvenation. This could be as simple as a five-minute meditation, a short walk, or time spent on a hobby.

Embracing Flexibility and Adaptability: Work-life balance isn't about evenly splitting hours between work and personal activities but finding a blend that aligns with your values and current life phase. Recognizing that some days or weeks will be more work-focused and others more personal-life-focused can help you manage your expectations and reduce stress.

Regular Reflection and Adjustment: I encourage you all to regularly reflect on your work-life balance and make adjustments as needed. Life's circumstances are always changing, and what worked one month may not be effective the next. Continuous reflection allows you to adapt your strategies to maintain a sense of balance in the moment.

Communication: Open communication with employers, colleagues, and family members about work-life balance needs can foster understanding and support.

By acknowledging that work-life balance is a fluid, ever-changing concept, you can better navigate the demands of your professional and personal lives without striving for an unattainable perfect balance. Instead, the focus should be on making conscious choices in the moment that align with your overall goals and well-being, understanding that these choices will evolve over time.

The Wider Impact

As we explore these strategies, we also consider the broader implications of Felicia's journey. Her story reflects a common struggle, highlighting the importance of practical, everyday approaches to managing stress and enhancing well-being. By demonstrating the tangible benefits of these simplified techniques, I want to inspire you to recognize and address your stressors to assist in fostering a more balanced, healthy, and fulfilling life. Through Felicia's experience, we highlight the significance of shedding unnecessary burdens and celebrating the courage it takes to prioritize one's overall health and happiness.

The Long-Term Consequences of the Weight of the Cape

The nuances of emotional health and physical well-being, particularly focusing on the concepts of somatic concerns and allostatic load, are crucial for understanding the long-term impacts of stress.

Enhanced Emotional Health Exploration

Emotional health is fundamental to overall well-being and is intricately connected to physical health. Over time, unaddressed emotional stress can lead to chronic conditions, affecting one's quality of life and capacity to cope with daily challenges.

1. Understanding Emotional Health: Emotional health involves more than just managing stress; it encompasses recognizing, expressing, and processing a wide range of emotions in a healthy way.

2. Impact of Chronic Stress on Emotional Health: Prolonged stress can lead to deep-seated emotional issues, such as anxiety, depression, and burnout, which can persist and evolve if not addressed.

3. Somatic Concerns: Emotional distress can manifest physically, leading to somatic symptoms. Stress can trigger physical symptoms like headaches, gastrointestinal issues, and chronic pain, which are not just symptoms but also stressors themselves, creating a feedback loop that exacerbates both emotional and physical strain.

Physical Well-being and Allostatic Load

Physical well-being is not just the absence of disease; it's the optimal functioning of all body systems. Chronic stress can disrupt this balance, leading to a concept known as allostatic load.

1. Your Allostatic Load: Your allostatic load is the cumulative burden of chronic stress and life demands on your body. It's the wear and tear that occurs when the body's stress response is activated too frequently or is not turned off adequately after a stressor is no longer present.

2. Consequences of High Allostatic Load: An elevated allostatic load can lead to various health issues, such as cardiovascular disease, diabetes, and weakened immune function. Your body's ability to regulate stress diminishes, which can exacerbate chronic conditions and increase susceptibility to new health problems.

3. Addressing Allostatic Load: To reduce your allostatic load, the importance of comprehensive stress management, regular physical activity, adequate sleep, nutritious diet, and mindfulness practices are key. These approaches help recalibrate the body's stress response, enhancing resilience and reducing the physical repercussions of stress.

Integrating Emotional and Physical Health Strategies

1. Holistic Approaches: A holistic approach to health that considers the interplay between emotional and physical well-being should be incorporated. Techniques like yoga, tai chi, and meditation can be particularly effective as they address both mental and physical aspects simultaneously.

2. Professional Guidance: For those struggling with somatic concerns or high allostatic load, I recommend seeking professional healthcare advice. Healthcare providers can offer tailored strategies to manage symptoms and underlying stressors, promoting a more balanced and healthful state.

3. Continuous Monitoring and Adjustment: Conduct regular self-assessment and professional check-ups to monitor both emotional and physical health. Early detection and intervention can prevent the escalation of stress-related health issues, promoting long-term well-being.

By understanding and addressing the complex connections between emotional health, somatic concerns, and your allostatic load, you can adopt more informed and effective strategies for maintaining health and vitality over the long term, ensuring a more balanced and fulfilling life journey.

Chapter 5: Embracing Vulnerability
Reflective Questions

1. How comfortable are you with being vulnerable and asking for help when needed?
2. Can you identify instances when vulnerability has led to deeper connections or personal growth?
3. What steps can you take to become more comfortable with vulnerability in your life?
4. How has fear of vulnerability influenced your relationships and decision-making?
5. In what ways can practicing vulnerability lead to greater authenticity and authenticity in your life?

Exercise 1: Reach out to a trusted friend or family member and share something vulnerable about yourself or your experiences. Reflect on their response and the impact of this act of vulnerability on your relationship.

Exercise 2: Create a list of three specific situations where you can practice vulnerability in the coming week. Implement these instances and journal about your feelings and experiences.

"She needed a hero, so that's what she became."
— Anonymous

CHAPTER 6

WHEN YOUR CAPE IS TATTERED FROM TRAUMA

As Addison sat in her therapist's office, she couldn't shake the feeling of being constantly on edge. Her heart raced, her palms were clammy, and a knot of anxiety twisted in her stomach. She had always prided herself on being strong and resilient: the epitome of the superwoman archetype. But lately, that cape felt more like a heavy burden than a symbol of empowerment.

As she recounted her experiences, tears welled in Addison's eyes. The trauma she had endured of physical and emotional abuse seemed to permeate every aspect of her life, leaving her feeling broken and disconnected. She had always strived to maintain an image of perfection to meet the expectations placed upon her by society, by her family, and by herself. But beneath the façade, she was struggling.

Her therapist listened with empathy, guiding her through the complexities of her emotions and experiences. Together, they explored how her developmental relational experiences and her trauma had created Addison's attachment style, as well as how they had influenced the way she formed and maintained relationships. Addison recognized herself in the descriptions of anxious-preoccupied attachment, constantly seeking reassurance, craving closeness, yet always fearing abandonment.

The trauma she had experienced had intensified these tendencies, magnifying her need for validation and connection while simultaneously heightening her fear of rejection and abandonment. This attachment style had become intricately woven into the fabric of her superwoman narrative, exacerbating her struggles with perfectionism and self-doubt.

As they delved deeper into attachment theory, Addison began to understand how her trauma had aggravated the challenges of the superwoman narrative. The relentless pressure to excel, to be everything to everyone, had only served to intensify her anxiety and diminish her sense of self-worth. Her therapist helped her see that it was okay to ask for help, to let down her guard, and to embrace vulnerability.

Together, they worked toward healing and reclaiming the frayed edges of Addison's metaphorical cape. Through therapy, she learned not only to set healthy boundaries but also to express her needs and desires in order to cultivate relationships built on mutual respect and understanding. It was a journey fraught with ups and downs, but with each step forward, Addison felt a little lighter, and a bit freer.

As she left her therapist's office that day, Addison knew she still had a long way to go. But for the first time in a long time, she felt hopeful. She was no longer defined by her trauma or constrained by the expectations of others. She was simply Addison, imperfect and flawed, but resilient and determined to rewrite her own narrative. And as she walked out into the world, she did so with a newfound sense of strength, her tattered cape fluttering behind her as a reminder of how far she had come.

The superwoman cape, initially a symbol of strength and resilience, can become tattered and worn when subjected to the weight of trauma. **The unique challenges that women face who have experienced trauma while wearing this metaphorical garment has to be addressed for healing and understanding to occur.** Trauma can have an impact on your daily levels of functioning, communication, stress, and anxiety levels. Trauma also has a profound influence on your attachment styles, which, in turn, impact the way you form and maintain relationships.

Trauma, in its various forms, leaves an indelible mark on those who endure it. When experienced while striving to meet the persistent expectations of the superwoman myth, the impact can be especially intense. The metaphorical cape that was once a symbol of empowerment may become a reminder of vulnerability and pain. This chapter seeks to shed light on the complex interplay between trauma, the superwoman narrative, and the way women navigate their interpersonal connections.

Trauma can encompass a wide range of experiences, from childhood adversity to intimate partner violence, from workplace discrimination to societal injustices. Regardless of its form, trauma can disrupt your sense of self, safety, and trust. When coupled with the expectations of being a superwoman, the emotional and psychological toll can be significant.

John Bowlby is the creator of attachment theory. He was a pioneer in understanding the emotional bond between infants and their primary caregivers, emphasizing the importance of these early relationships in shaping an individual's social and emotional development throughout life. This theory delineates how the nature of these early bonds, particularly the quality of care and responsiveness from caregivers, forms the basis for "attachment styles"—patterns of relating to others that persist into adulthood. Bowlby's work suggests that secure attachments in infancy foster confidence and self-esteem, whereas insecure attachments can lead to challenges in trust and self-worth as individuals grow.

Attachment Styles and Trauma Responses

Attachment theory classifies attachment styles into four primary categories:

1. Secure Attachment: Individuals with secure attachment styles tend to have caregivers who consistently meet their emotional and physical needs. These individuals typically have a positive view of themselves and others in relationships. Securely attached individuals feel comfortable with intimacy

and independence, strike a healthy balance in relationships, and can manage conflicts constructively.

2. Anxious-Preoccupied Attachment: Those with an anxious-preoccupied attachment style often seek high levels of closeness and are concerned about their partner's availability. They may be prone to jealousy and require frequent reassurance to feel secure in relationships.

3. Dismissive-Avoidant Attachment: People with a dismissive-avoidant attachment style prioritize independence and may struggle with emotional reliance on others. They often come across as emotionally distant and have difficulty with vulnerability.

4. Fearful-Avoidant Attachment (Disorganized Attachment): The fearful-avoidant attachment style is characterized by a mix of anxious and avoidant behaviors. Individuals with this style may have difficulty trusting others and navigating the emotional complexities of relationships. They may vacillate between a desire for closeness and a fear of vulnerability.

Impact of Trauma on Attachment Styles and Relationships

Trauma can significantly influence these attachment styles, shaping how individuals respond to stress and adversity in relationships. Here's how trauma impacts each attachment style:

1. Trauma and Anxious-Preoccupied Attachment: Trauma often leads to heightened anxiety, hypervigilance in relationships, and an increased need for reassurance and closeness. This attachment style may exacerbate the challenges of the superwoman narrative, as trauma survivors may struggle with trust and have intense emotional reactions to perceived threats in their quest for perfection.

2. Trauma and Dismissive-Avoidant Attachment: Trauma survivors may emotionally distance themselves as a protective mechanism, especially when facing overwhelming emotions or vulnerability. This distancing can

manifest as a reluctance to rely on others for support and a preference for handling emotions independently.

3. Trauma and Fearful-Avoidant Attachment: Trauma can intensify the inner conflict and confusion experienced by individuals with this attachment style, making it challenging to trust others and navigate complex emotional dynamics in relationships.

Clinical Implications and Relevance to the Superwoman Narrative

Understanding attachment theory and its intersection with trauma is essential for clinicians working with women who grapple with the superwoman narrative. Trauma-informed approaches should take into account individuals' attachment styles, as these styles profoundly influence their responses to relationships and self-perception. Addison found herself contending with the fraying of her superwoman cape after experiencing a traumatic event. Once confident in her ability to meet the world's demands, trauma shattered her sense of invincibility, leaving her struggling with post-traumatic stress and overwhelming anxiety. Addison's attachment style changed over time based on life experiences—just like the shape of her cape.

Addison's story embodies the profound impact that trauma can have on the superwoman narrative. Her experience highlights how the metaphorical cape, once a symbol of strength, can become a source of distress when subjected to the weight of traumatic events. Trauma, in all its manifestations, has the power to unravel the sense of invulnerability that often accompanies the superwoman persona.

For many women like Addison, the struggle to maintain the superwoman disguise becomes even more challenging in the aftermath of trauma. The expectations placed upon women by society, the workplace, and sometimes even themselves can feel suffocating when layered upon the emotional scars left by traumatic events. The cape that once represented empowerment can start to fray and tear, symbolizing vulnerability rather than strength.

Chapter 6: Setting Realistic Expectations
Reflective Questions

1. How do you think you attach in Relationships?

2. How have relationships helped or hurt your overall well-being?

3. How has trauma impacted your life?

4. What measures have you taken to heal?

5. What steps can you take to work toward healing your trauma and becoming more secure?

Exercise 1: Identify the patterns you have in your relationships both healthy and unhealthy and write about what you are willing to do to have a different outcome.

Exercise 2: Write a letter to yourself, celebrating who you are and give yourself permission to do whatever it takes to take the necessary step to begin your healing journey.

"Throw me to the wolves and I will return leading the pack."
— Suzanne Collins

CHAPTER 7

TRYING TO DRESS UP THE CAPE

Brielle strides into the sleek, modern confines of the architectural studio each morning, her heels clicking against the polished concrete floor. The space hums with creative energy, as designers huddle around drafting tables and computers, their heads bent in focused concentration. Brielle is no exception, her mind already buzzing with ideas for her latest project.

As a seasoned architect, Brielle has earned a reputation for her innovative designs and meticulous attention to detail. She relishes the challenge of bringing her clients' visions to life, transforming abstract concepts into tangible structures that inspire awe and admiration. But with each new project comes a fresh wave of pressure, the weight of her cape growing heavier with every passing day.

Brielle's days unfold in a whirlwind of activity, each one filled with client meetings, design reviews, and project deadlines. She juggles multiple tasks simultaneously, her calendar overflowing with appointments and obligations. Yet, **no matter how carefully she plans her schedule, there never seems to be enough time to accomplish everything on her plate.**

In the midst of the chaos, Brielle finds solace at her drafting table, where she loses herself in the rhythm of pencil on paper. Here, amidst the soft glow of her desk lamp, she feels a sense of peace wash over her, a respite from the relentless demands of her profession. But even as she immerses herself in her work, the weight of her cape remains a constant presence—a reminder of the expectations she must meet.

Client meetings are a frequent occurrence in Brielle's world, each one a high-stakes affair filled with anticipation and anxiety. She presents her designs with confidence, her words flowing smoothly as she articulates her vision to her clients. Yet, beneath the surface, Brielle wrestles with a nagging fear that she's not good enough and that her designs will fall short of expectations.

As the hours stretch into the evening, Brielle remains in the studio, the soft glow of her computer screen casting long shadows across the room. The rest of the world fades away as she loses herself in her work, the lines between day and night blurring into obscurity. But even as she pours herself into her designs, the weight of her cape grows heavier with each passing moment: a constant reminder of the burden she carries.

Despite the exhaustion that threatens to consume her, Brielle soldiers on, driven by a continual determination to succeed. She knows that she must keep pushing forward and that she must continue to strive for excellence even in the face of adversity. Brielle finally goes home for the night and shuts down for the evening. She wakes up the next morning and pulls tags off of a new dress to wear to make her feel better. Brielle then adds extra steps to her makeup routine and slides into her favorite stilettos—all in the name of dressing up the cape.

Brielle copes with her stress by masking it with a veneer of perfection and poise. Despite the increasing pressures of her career, she maintains an impeccable exterior, using her wardrobe and demeanor as a shield to conceal her growing anxieties and the toll they take on her well-being.

Each morning, Brielle stands before her wardrobe, carefully selecting the day's armor. Her choices aren't just about fashion; they're strategic decisions meant to project strength and competence. The meticulous application of makeup is equally deliberate, serving to obscure the fatigue etched beneath her eyes from countless late-night working sessions. This ritual is less about vanity and more about crafting a persona that can face the world's expectations without flinching. It's her way of reinforcing the ramparts, preparing to meet the day's challenges with a façade that feels increasingly at odds with her inner conflict.

At the architectural studio, Brielle's exterior radiates confidence and control, yet internally, she's contending with an endless stream of deadlines and client demands. Her interactions are measured, her smile practiced, yet each nod and handshake bring a growing sense of being overwhelmed. The juxtaposition of her polished appearance against the chaos of her mind creates a conflict that she struggles to reconcile. Despite her achievements and the respect she commands within her field, Brielle wrestles with the nagging doubt that she could be doing more, performing better, and living up to an ideal that seems ever out of reach.

"Dressing Up the Cape" explores the sustainability of the approach that many women take within their lives, questioning how long one can maintain this coverup before the stress manifests in more tangible ways. It's a reflection of the balance between professional dedication and personal well-being, highlighting the importance of acknowledging and addressing the underlying pressures rather than merely disguising them. The narrative probes the potential repercussions of ignoring your needs, suggesting that the armor/cape you and your sisters on each day might protect you from external judgments but not from the internal consequences of unaddressed stress.

As the chapter concludes, there's a need of introspection from women, a growing realization that while the external armor might shield us from immediate scrutiny, it doesn't alleviate the underlying stress. This introspective moment is a turning point, offering a glimmer of recognition that perhaps true strength lies in vulnerability and authenticity. It sets the stage for a potential journey toward reconciling your inner world with your outer presentation, hinting at a future where you and Brielle might find a way to reconfigure the cape rather than merely dress it up.

Chapter 7: Balancing Multiple Roles
Reflective Questions

1. How do you currently balance multiple roles in your life, and how satisfied are you with this balance?
2. Can you identify any role conflicts or challenges that arise when juggling various responsibilities?
3. What strategies have you used in the past to manage and prioritize your roles effectively?
4. How can aligning your roles with your values lead to a more balanced and fulfilling life?
5. What support systems or resources can enhance your ability to balance multiple roles?

Exercise 1: Create a visual representation of the various roles you play in your life using a diagram or mind map. Reflect on how these roles interact and overlap.

Exercise 2: Identify one role in your life that feels out of balance. Develop a plan to realign this role with your values and priorities. Implement the plan and journal about your progress.

"Your willingness to look at your darkness is what empowers you to change."
– Iyanla Vanzant

CHAPTER 8

THE CAPE AS YOUR KRYPTONITE

In the bustling environment of her gourmet restaurant, Rhonda stands out not just for her exceptional culinary skills but also as a woman in a high-pressure, male-dominated cooking world. Her day begins before dawn, as she meticulously plans her menu, sourcing the finest ingredients to ensure each dish meets her exacting standards. Despite her accomplishments and the innovation she brings to her cuisine, Rhonda faces an uphill battle for recognition and respect. Her ideas and leadership are often scrutinized more harshly than those of her male counterparts, compelling her to constantly validate her expertise and authority in the kitchen. This scrutiny extends beyond her professional environment, affecting her interactions at industry events, where her achievements are sometimes overshadowed by her gender. The pressure to continuously prove herself in the culinary world is a relentless challenge, yet Rhonda remains undeterred. With every dish she perfects and every accolade she earns, she's not only solidifying her reputation but also paving the way for future female chefs to rise and be recognized for their talent, not their gender.

Zoe's world is one of deep-sea exploration and marine conservation, where she's more at home among the waves and wildlife than adhering to societal expectations on land. Her choice to prioritize her career in oceanography over more traditional roles is met with a mix of admiration and skepticism. Friends, family, and even strangers often question her decision to remain child-free, implying that her achievements and contributions to science somehow lack fulfillment without motherhood. Undaunted, Zoe continues her research, contributing valuable insights into marine ecosystems and advocating for the preservation of our oceans. Her work, often solitary and demanding, is driven by a passion for discovery and a deep sense of purpose. Zoe's journey is a powerful narrative of self-determination, illustrating that a woman's worth and identity are defined by her choices, aspirations, and contributions to the world, not by conforming to prescribed societal roles.

Both Rhonda and Zoe exemplify the strength it takes to stand firm in one's convictions in the face of societal expectations. Their stories, while unique in their settings and challenges, converge on the theme of resilience. They embody the essence of women everywhere who are breaking barriers, challenging norms, and redefining what it means to be successful and fulfilled. Through their narratives, we discover the diverse ways women navigate and resist the pressures imposed by societal expectations, serving as a beacon of empowerment and self-realization.

In the world of superheroes, kryptonite is not just a physical substance but also a potent symbol of vulnerability, representing the internal and external forces that weaken even the strongest of individuals. Similarly, for Rhonda and Zoe, **the pressures and demands of societal expectations act as their own forms of kryptonite, threatening to undermine their confidence and resilience.** For Rhonda, the constant scrutiny and gender biases she faces in the culinary world serve as her kryptonite, chipping away at her self-assurance and causing her to doubt her abilities. Despite her undeniable talent and dedication, she is forced to expend precious energy defending her expertise and proving her worth, leaving her feeling drained and vulnerable. Meanwhile, Zoe's decision to prioritize her career over traditional notions of femininity and motherhood exposes her to judgment and criticism from those who question her choices. The societal pressure to conform to predefined roles and expectations weighs heavily on her, threatening to erode her sense of self-worth and purpose.

Just as kryptonite weakens superheroes, the expectations imposed by society can diminish the strength and resolve of women like Rhonda and Zoe. Yet, despite these challenges, they refuse to be defined by the limitations imposed upon them. Instead, they draw upon their inner determination to confront their kryptonite head-on, refusing to let it dictate the course of their lives. Rhonda and Zoe struggle to navigate the treacherous waters of societal expectations, forging their paths with courage and conviction.

As women, we all have moments where our very own kryptonite may weaken us temporarily, it is our inner strength and determination that ultimately prevail, allowing us to both rise above the limitations imposed upon us and embrace our true potential.

Unspoken Expectations and Their Impact

In addition to the overt challenges Rhonda and Zoe face, there exists a subtler yet equally challenging foe: the unspoken expectations society places on women. These expectations, ingrained in cultural norms and reinforced through media, subtly dictate how women should look, behave, and navigate the world. They are the silent rules that govern everything from appearance to career choices, often manifesting in subtle forms of bias and discrimination.

For Rhonda, the unspoken expectation is that her success in the culinary world should not overshadow her duties as a woman. Despite her professional achievements, there's an underlying pressure for her to conform to traditional gender roles, balancing her career ambitions with societal expectations of domesticity and nurturing. This expectation, while seldom explicitly stated, adds an extra layer of complexity to Rhonda's already demanding journey, forcing her to juggle not only the pressures of her profession but also the weight of societal norms.

Similarly, Zoe grapples with implicit expectations about womanhood and femininity in her field of oceanography. The assumption that women should prioritize family over career and adhere to traditional roles as caregivers creates an invisible barrier for Zoe, subtly undermining her choices and contributions. Despite her groundbreaking research and dedication to marine conservation, Zoe is often judged not only for her professional decisions but also for her personal ones, as society questions her commitment to traditional notions of femininity.

Over time, these unspoken expectations take a toll on Rhonda and Zoe, both physically and emotionally. The constant pressure to meet societal standards, to balance career aspirations with personal responsibilities, and to navigate biases and stereotypes wears them down, leaving them feeling exhausted and depleted. Physically, they may experience symptoms of stress and burnout fatigue, insomnia, and muscle tension. Emotionally, they may struggle with feelings of inadequacy, impostor syndrome, and depression, as they struggle with the ongoing demands placed upon them.

Yet, despite these challenges, Rhonda and Zoe persevere, drawing upon their inner strength to defy societal expectations and carve out their paths on their terms. Their stories serve as a powerful reminder of the resilience and resolve of women everywhere who confront and challenge the unspoken expectations imposed upon them, refusing to be confined by limitations or stereotypes.

My hope is that, for you, Rhonda and Zoe's stories offer solidarity and inspiration. May their accounts encourage you to resist societal expectations, prioritize your well-being, and challenge the norms that seek to confine you. By embracing your authenticity and reclaiming your agency, you can transcend the limitations imposed upon you, reshaping the narrative for women everywhere. Wear your cape with pride, for your story is a testament to your fortitude.

Chapter 8: Navigating Workplace Challenges
Reflective Questions

1. How have workplace expectations and biases affected your career and job satisfaction?
2. Can you recall specific incidents or patterns of workplace challenges related to societal norms and biases?
3. What strategies have you used to combat workplace biases and stereotypes?
4. How can greater awareness of these challenges empower you in your career?
5. In what ways can advocating for change in workplace attitudes benefit both you and future generations of women?

Exercise 1: Document instances of workplace challenges related to societal expectations and biases. Reflect on how you responded and identify alternative strategies for handling similar situations in the future.

Exercise 2: Engage in a self-affirmation practice before or after work to boost your self-confidence and resilience in the face of workplace challenges. Track how this practice influences your mindset over time.

"She is a little wildflower with a lot of warrior underneath."
– Melody Lee

CHAPTER 9

THE RED, WHITE, AND BLUE CAPE

In the multifaceted realm of military service, Command Sergeant Major Ava Mitchell emerges as a beacon of resilience and grit, her narrative woven from the threads of loyalty, duty, respect, selfless service, honor, integrity, and personal courage. Straight out of high school, Command Sergeant Major Mitchell was accepted into the revered ranks of the United States Army, her heart ablaze with the same fervent patriotism that had coursed through the veins of her family for generations. Raised in a household steeped in military tradition, Ava was no stranger to the call of duty; it was a melody that had sung her to sleep since childhood, a legacy that pulsed within her with the cadence of a steady drumbeat.

As Command Sergeant Major Mitchell stepped onto the hallowed grounds of military training, she found herself thrust into a world of discipline, camaraderie, and unyielding perseverance. Days blurred into nights as she honed her skills, forged bonds of brotherhood and sisterhood, and embraced the profound sense of purpose that came with donning the uniform. Yet, amidst the ceaseless rhythm of military life, there existed a silent symphony—the gentle pressures of motherhood.

For Command Sergeant Major Mitchell, the journey of military service was not one traversed alone but intertwined intimately with the joys and challenges of raising a family. With children in tow, she navigated the convoluted corridors of duty and responsibility, her days punctuated by the tender embrace of her little ones and the resolute call to serve her nation. Deployments meant not only bidding farewell to the comfort of home but also to the laughter and innocence that danced in the eyes of her children.

Balancing the demands of a military career with the nurturing embrace of motherhood posed a difficult challenge for Command Sergeant Major Mitchell. The weight of her red, white, and blue cape bore down upon her shoulders, its threads woven from the fabric of sacrifice and dedication. Yet, along with the tumult of deployments and training exercises, Command Sergeant Major Mitchell found solace in the knowledge that every sacrifice made in service to her country was a legacy she bestowed upon her children—a testament to the values of courage, honor, and resilience that defined their family lineage.

There is a delicate interplay of duty and family that Command Sergeant Major Mitchell and many women struggle with when trying to achieve excellence amidst the tender embrace of motherhood. For Command Sergeant Major Mitchell, the superwoman cape was not merely a symbol but a lived reality, a mantle she wears with pride and determination, a tribute to the indomitable spirit of women who dare to serve both their country and their families with grace and valor.

It is important that we shift our focus to the remarkable women who have chosen to serve or have served in the military, all while shouldering the heavy burden of the red, white, and blue superwoman cape. These women exemplify true superheroes, navigating a complex and multifaceted web of challenges, sacrifices, and extraordinary successes that are inherently unique to their chosen path. Their stories are a testament to strength, bravery, and steadfast commitment, shedding light on the weighty intersection of military service and societal expectations.

The women who serve or have served in the military have embraced a calling that demands courage beyond measure. They have made a conscious choice to dedicate themselves to a life of service, often in the face of extreme challenges. These challenges encompass not only the physical and mental demands of military training and deployments but also the intricate balance they must strike between their roles as soldiers and the societal expectations that surround them as women.

The intersection of military service and societal expectations brings to light a wide range of topics, including issues related to gender equity, mental health, family dynamics, and personal identity. We will explore the challenges these women face, such as the pressures to conform to traditional feminine roles, the balance between military duty and personal life, and the resilience required to overcome adversity in male-dominated environments.

Additionally, I want to celebrate the triumphs and achievements of these women, highlighting their invaluable contributions to their countries and the world. Their stories serve as an inspiration to all, demonstrating that the superwoman cape is not just symbolic but a tangible reality for those who serve.

The Dual Commitment: Service and Family

Command Sergeant Major Mitchell's life showcases the unique challenges faced by women who simultaneously navigate the demanding worlds of military service and family life. For these women, the superwoman cape takes on a patriotic hue, reflecting the red, white, and blue of the American flag, symbolizing their strong commitment to both the nation and their families.

Command Sergeant Major Mitchell's expedition is emblematic of the countless military women who confront the intricate balance of their dual commitments. Their experiences epitomize the internal conflict that women often encounter in male-dominated arenas. Here, the superwoman cape becomes a powerful representation of their extraordinary ability to fulfill these dual roles.

Balancing the demands of military service, which include deployments, rigorous training, and long hours, with the equally challenging roles of motherhood, partnership, and maintaining a household is a monumental task. Military women like you, someone you may know, or Command Sergeant Major Mitchell face a unique set of challenges that require unparalleled resilience and adaptability.

The emotional struggle experienced is intense. On one hand, they are dedicated to their military duties where they often have to prove themselves in a male-dominated environment. They navigate a world where gender biases may persist, and they must continually demonstrate their competence and capabilities. On the other hand, they are equally devoted to their families, striving to be present, nurturing, and supportive partners and mothers.

This balancing act often involves making difficult choices, such as managing deployments while ensuring the well-being of their children and maintaining strong relationships with their spouses. It also entails coping with the emotional toll of being separated from their families during military assignments.

Despite these challenges, women like you, or someone you may know, and Command Sergeant Major Mitchell persevere. They excel in their military careers, break through barriers, and set inspiring examples for future generations of female service members. The collective stories underscore the profound strength required to carry the dual commitment of serving the country and nurturing families, all while wearing the red, white, and blue cape of dedication and sacrifice.

In highlighting the experiences of these extraordinary women, we gain insight into the complexities of their lives and the emotional struggle they must navigate. The stories inspire us to appreciate the tremendous sacrifices made as well as recognize the steadfast dedication to both the nation and their families. Command Sergeant Major Mitchell, you and your counterparts demonstrate that the superwoman cape, in all its patriotic glory, is not just a symbol but a lived reality for those who proudly serve and nurture your loved ones.

Challenges and Sacrifices: The Struggles Beneath the Cape

I would be remiss if I did not delve into the many challenges and sacrifices faced by servicewomen, often concealed beneath the superwoman cape they wear. While their dedication to both military service and family responsibilities remains unfaltering, many women endure a multitude of struggles that often go unnoticed.

Deployments, a fundamental aspect of military service, can take servicewomen away from their families for extended and emotionally taxing periods. The toll on both the women in service and their loved ones can be immense. Children may experience the absence of their mothers during crucial developmental stages, spouses struggle with the daunting responsibilities of solo parenting, and servicewomen themselves confront the emotional turmoil of separation from their families.

The emotional challenges experienced by servicewomen and their families are numerous. The sacrifices made during deployments, the missed birthdays, anniversaries, and milestones, all contribute to a complex web of emotions. These women carry the weight of their responsibilities and the longing for their families as they fulfill their duty to their nation.

Beyond the emotional challenges, there are the physically demanding aspects of military service that servicewomen must navigate. Many undergo rigorous training, demonstrating their physical prowess, all while continuing to fulfill their roles as caregivers and partners. The sheer balancing act of excelling in their military careers while maintaining their responsibilities on the home front is a notable testament to their inner strength. The physical demands of military service, such as maintaining fitness standards and participating in challenging training exercises, can be particularly grueling. Servicewomen often find themselves pushing the limits of their physical capabilities, not only to meet the requirements of their roles but also to prove their competence and dedication in male-dominated military environments.

In addition to these challenges, servicewomen may encounter unique obstacles related to their gender, including biases, stereotypes, and potential harassment or discrimination. These additional hurdles further underline the immense strength and determination required to thrive in military service while donning the superwoman cape and tarnishing the bright red, white and blue of their capes.

Despite the often-hidden struggles and sacrifices many endure, servicewomen continue to persevere, serving their nation with unparalleled dedication and courage. Their stories serve as a poignant reminder of the toughness, determination, and indomitable spirit that define them. It is through their experiences that we gain a deeper appreciation for the true magnitude of their contributions and the extraordinary strength it takes to carry the dual commitment of serving their country and nurturing their families while wearing the superwoman cape.

Remarkable Successes: Triumphs Beneath the Cape

In the face of incredible challenges and sacrifices, servicewomen demonstrate their amazing resilience and capacity for success. Their significant achievements shine brilliantly beneath the weight of their capes, serving as powerful testaments to their unwavering dedication and exceptional abilities.

One of the most remarkable aspects of these servicewomen's journeys is their ability to shatter stereotypes and break down barriers in the traditionally male-dominated military world. Colonel Camila Ramirez's story is a shining example. She soared to become the high ranking Latina officer in the U.S. Air Force, an incredible achievement that signifies her exceptional leadership and dedication. Colonel Ramirez's success not only serves as a personal triumph but also as an inspiration to countless others, proving that women are more than capable of reaching the highest echelons of military leadership.

Moreover, many servicewomen excel in their military careers, earning accolades and commendations for their bravery, competence, and dedication to their duty. Their accomplishments serve as beacons of inspiration, not only to their fellow servicemembers but also to future generations of women who aspire to wear the uniform.

These women demonstrate time and again that gender is no barrier to success. They showcase their exceptional leadership skills, intelligence, physical prowess, and firm commitment to their country. They lead troops into battle, make critical decisions, and contribute significantly to the safety and security of their nations.

Their accomplishments remind us of the boundless potential that lies within every woman. They show that women can excel in any field they choose, whether it's in military service, science, business, arts, or any other domain. Women are not limited by societal expectations or stereotypes; instead, they defy these constraints and rise to the occasion, achieving greatness and leaving an indelible mark on history.

These servicewomen's stories of remarkable success inspire us to celebrate the outstanding capabilities of women and to recognize that there are no limits to what they can achieve. They serve as a strong reminder that women are not defined by their gender but by their determination, resilience, and dedication. Through their accomplishments, these women pave the way for a more inclusive world where opportunities are based on merit and not on gender, inspiring generations of women to reach for the stars, achieve their dreams, and stand proudly with their red, white, and blue capes.

The Intersection of Duty, Challenges, and Successes

The intersection of duty, challenges, and noteworthy successes is where the red, white, and blue cape truly comes to life. Servicewomen, who wear this cape, embody heroism not only in their military roles but also within the walls of their homes and throughout their communities. This chapter serves as a tribute to their stories, illuminating the extraordinary achievements they attain and the formidable challenges they confront with extreme determination.

It is essential to recognize that servicewomen are heroes in uniform. They make the courageous choice to serve their countries, often facing daunting and life-threatening situations. Their commitment to duty is tireless, and they put themselves on the line to protect and defend their nations. These women demonstrate valor, fortitude, and unparalleled dedication to a cause larger than themselves.

But their heroism extends far beyond their military service. Servicewomen are also heroes in their homes where they juggle the dual roles of serving and caregiving. They navigate the complexities of maintaining strong family bonds while being separated from their loved ones during deployments or rigorous training exercises. The sacrifices they make and the emotional strength they exhibit within their households are awe-inspiring.

Furthermore, servicewomen are heroes within their communities. They often engage in outreach programs, volunteer work, and support initiatives that benefit society at large. Their dedication to making a positive impact on the lives of others exemplifies their commitment to service, not just on the battlefield but in all aspects of life.

This chapter aims to shine a spotlight on the amazing women who embody this intersection of duty, challenges, and successes. Their stories serve as a testament to the indomitable spirit of women who embrace their responsibilities with grace and determination. Through their remarkable achievements, servicewomen break barriers, shatter stereotypes, and inspire not only their fellow servicemembers but also future generations of women.

Their stories remind us that, as extraordinary women, we are capable of achieving greatness in every facet of life. They show that women have the resilience to overcome challenges, the courage to face adversity, and the compassion to make a positive impact on the world. Servicewomen exemplify the idea that heroes come in all forms and that gender should never be a limitation to pursuing one's dreams and making a difference.

In closing, **let us extend our heartfelt admiration and gratitude to the remarkable women who serve their communities and our nation with**

incredible dedication and courage. Your selfless contributions, strength in the face of adversity, and pledge to the greater good inspire us all. As we reflect on your invaluable service, we salute your unwavering strength and commitment to making the world a better place for us all.

Chapter 9: The Red, White, and Blue Cape
Those That Serve or Have Served in the Military
Reflective Questions

1. How does military service intersect with societal expectations, and what unique challenges does it present?
2. Can you imagine the dual commitment of serving in the military while fulfilling family responsibilities?
3. What sacrifices do servicewomen make, and how can these sacrifices impact their well-being and relationships?
4. What remarkable successes have servicewomen achieved, and how do they inspire you?
5. How can society better support and appreciate the contributions of women in the military?

Exercise 1: Write a letter of appreciation to a servicewoman or veteran, acknowledging their dedication and sacrifices. Consider sending it to a military support organization or directly to a servicewoman you know.

Exercise 2: Reflect on a challenging situation in your own life where you had to balance dual commitments. Apply the resilience strategies discussed in previous chapters to address the situation more effectively.

"Everyone could use some couch time."
– Gigi Hamilton

CHAPTER 10

THE CAPE ESCAPE

Cora is a dedicated certified public accountant (CPA) navigating the fast-paced world of a bustling accounting firm. Her days are a blur of deadlines, client meetings, and endless spreadsheets, each task demanding her full attention and expertise. As a perfectionist by nature, Cora takes pride in her ability to excel in her career while still managing the responsibilities of home and family.

Yet, beneath the appearance of competence lies a woman stretched thin by the weight of her responsibilities. Cora begins to experience symptoms of burnout—a persistent sense of exhaustion, emotional detachment, and a growing sense of cynicism toward her work. She finds herself struggling to concentrate, her once sharp mind now fogged by fatigue and stress. The relentless demands of her career leave little time for self-care or meaningful connection with loved ones.

Amidst the chaos of her life, Cora reaches a breaking point. Overwhelmed by feelings of exhaustion and despair, she finds herself unable to summon the energy to face another day at the office. It is a moment of profound vulnerability as she confronts the harsh reality that she can no longer continue to function as she has.

In the depths of her despair, Cora experiences a moment of clarity—a recognition that she has been carrying the weight of the superwoman cape for far too long. It is a pivotal moment in her voyage as she begins to see the possibility of a different path forward. With newfound resolve, she sets out on a journey of self-discovery and transformation, determined to reclaim her authenticity and sense of self-worth.

Cora's story serves as an important reminder that success is not measured solely by professional achievements but by the ability to live striving for a fulfilling life. As we travel alongside Cora, we are invited to reflect on our own struggles and breakthroughs, recognizing the importance of self-compassion and authenticity in a world that often demands perfection.

In Cora's passage from burnout to breakthrough, we find inspiration to redefine our priorities and forge a path toward well-being and fulfillment. It is a reminder that true success is not found in the relentless pursuit of perfection but in the courage to embrace our imperfections and prioritize what truly matters.

The silent suffering that countless women endure beneath the weight of the superwoman cape is a burden often hidden from the outside world. This emotional toll can be very overwhelming as you strive to excel in your careers, maintain meaningful relationships, and uphold your roles as caregivers. This emotional burden frequently manifests as anxiety, depression, and a continual sense of inadequacy, becoming constant companions within your life travels.

The superwoman cape, while symbolizing strength and resilience, also conceals a hidden struggle. It represents the belief that you can, and should, manage it all—a demanding career, a loving family, a nurturing home, and societal expectations of perfection. However, as the weight of these expectations bears down, the silent suffering begins. It's a suffering that often goes unnoticed, masked by smiles and a pretense of competence, leaving you to grapple with your inner turmoil in isolation.

There are countless ways in which women carry the weight of the cape and the psychological cost it exacts. There exists a complex interplay of societal pressures, personal aspirations, and the unrelenting pursuit of an idealized version of womanhood. The emotional toll of wearing the superwoman cape can manifest in various forms. Anxiety can become a constant companion as you strive to meet the high standards set forth in both your personal and professional lives. Depression may creep in as you contend with the overwhelming demands placed upon you, and you struggle to find moments of respite and self-care. The persistent sense of inadequacy, driven by the fear of falling short in any aspect of your lives, can erode self-esteem and self-worth.

This chapter is not just about suffering; it is about recognizing the silent struggle and the need for change. It explores the awakening that occurs when you realize that you cannot continue to bear the weight of the superwoman cape without consequences to your mental and emotional well-being. It is a journey toward self-discovery, self-compassion, and the understanding that asking for help is not a sign of weakness but a courageous act of self-preservation.

This is an invitation for you to explore the emotional landscape that many women navigate in their quest to manage it all. It encourages reflection on the toll of societal expectations and the realization that something must change. I want to offer you a path toward healing, self-acceptance, and the discovery of a more satisfying way of living that doesn't require the constant pressure of a superwoman cape.

Silent Suffering: The Overwhelming Emotional Weight

Beneath the façade of strength and perfection, many women have to deal with the ongoing burden of silent suffering. The emotional cost of constantly striving to meet societal expectations can become an oppressive weight that feels increasingly heavy over time. Anxiety, like an unwelcome visitor, creeps in, casting long shadows on their self-worth and daily functioning.

Depression lurks in the corners of their minds, often going unrecognized by those around them. The constant sense of inadequacy becomes an insistent companion, a weight that they carry with them daily, as they try to manage it all.

The emotional challenges that women experience under the weight of the superwoman cape are deeply ingrained in the fabric of their lives. As they strive to excel in their careers, maintain meaningful relationships, and fulfill their roles as caregivers, they often internalize the pressure to do it all flawlessly. The constant pursuit of this elusive perfection takes a toll on their mental and emotional well-being.

Anxiety is a frequent and unwelcome guest in the lives of many women. It manifests as a constant worry that they will fall short in some aspect of their lives. The fear of not meeting the high standards set by society can be paralyzing. This anxiety may manifest in various forms, from general unease to panic attacks, and it can have a serious impact on a woman's ability to function effectively in both the workplace and personal life.

Depression, too, is a shadow that often haunts the minds of women who silently suffer. The overwhelming weight of their responsibilities and the persistent feeling of inadequacy can lead to feelings of hopelessness and despair. Unfortunately, depression often goes unrecognized because women are adept at concealing their emotional struggles behind a veneer of competence and strength.

To illustrate the depth of silent suffering, let's jump right into Shonda's story.

Shonda had always been the pillar of support for her friends and family. She seemed invincible, seamlessly juggling her demanding job, caring for her aging parents, and ensuring her children had the best opportunities. However, behind closed doors, the weight of her superwoman cape became unbearable. One day, she found herself overwhelmed by anxiety, unable to get out of bed. It was her breaking point, the moment when she realized she couldn't continue to carry the weight any longer. Shonda's story reflects the silent suffering that so many women endure as they try to meet the impossibly high standards placed upon them.

The clinical impact of this type of distress is acute. It can lead to the development of anxiety disorders, depressive disorders, and a range of physical health issues, including sleep disturbances, chronic stress, and even cardiovascular problems. In the workplace, the emotional burden can result in decreased productivity, burnout, and a lack of fulfillment in one's career.

Recognizing long-term problems and addressing silent suffering is crucial for the well-being of women. It involves acknowledging the toll of societal expectations, seeking support, and promoting self-compassion. By shedding light on the emotional weight that many women carry and providing avenues for support and healing, we can collectively work toward a more compassionate and understanding society that values the well-being of women as much as their achievements.

Moments of Clarity: Revelations and External Catalysts

Moments of clarity are transformative experiences that hold the power to reshape your life, allowing you to break free from the suffocating weight of the superwoman cape. These moments are as diverse as the women who experience them, representing profound revelations, epiphanies, or external catalysts that trigger a shift in perspective and prompt a reevaluation of life's priorities and values.

Profound Revelations and Epiphanies: Some women experience moments of clarity as insightful revelations that lead to a fundamental shift in thinking. These revelations often come from deep introspection or personal growth experiences. They can be as simple as recognizing that you deserve happiness and fulfillment, or as complex as realizing that the pursuit of perfection is an unattainable and detrimental goal. These epiphanies empower you to acknowledge that you can choose a different path, one that aligns with your true values and well-being. It is a moment of self-discovery and self-acceptance, allowing you to shed the expectations that have bound you to the superwoman cape.

External Catalysts: For others, moments of clarity arise in response to external pressures or life-changing events. These catalysts can take the form of a health scare, a relationship breakdown, the death of a loved one, or professional burnout. When faced with such challenges, you are often forced to confront the limitations of the superwoman cape and the toll it has taken on your physical and emotional health. These external catalysts serve as wake-up calls, prompting you to reevaluate your lives with a heightened sense of urgency. You realize that continuing on the same path may lead to further anguish, and you seek a more balanced and sustainable way of living.

In both cases, moments of clarity are transformative because they lead to a reexamination of priorities and values. You begin to question whether the relentless pursuit of perfection and the need to manage it all are worth the sacrifices to your well-being. You will begin to understand that true strength lies in recognizing your limits and embracing self-care, self-compassion, and the pursuit of happiness and fulfillment.

These moments of clarity also empower you to make courageous decisions and take concrete steps toward change. **You may choose to redefine your career goals, establish healthier boundaries in your relationships, prioritize self-care, and seek professional help to address your emotional well-being. These actions represent a significant departure from the superwoman narrative, emphasizing self-empowerment and self-care as essential components of a fulfilling life.**

Moments of clarity are pivotal turning points in the lives of women who have worn the superwoman cape. They provide opportunities for self-discovery, self-acceptance, and the reevaluation of priorities. These moments serve as catalysts for change, prompting you to free yourself from the weight of unrealistic expectations and societal pressures. By acknowledging the power of these moments and supporting others in their path toward self-empowerment and well-being, we can contribute to a more compassionate and well-adjusted society that values the mental and emotional health of women as much as our achievements.

The Courage to Seek Help: Embracing Vulnerability

Recognizing the need for change is a significant and courageous step, but it often comes with a deep sense of vulnerability. Women who arrive at the point of realizing that it's time for something different must summon tremendous courage to seek help and support. This might involve reaching out to therapists, professional coaches, support groups, or other sources of assistance as they begin their life-changing journey. Your willingness to embrace vulnerability and ask for help is a profound testament to your strength and determination to break free from the constraints of the superwoman myth.

Recognizing the Need for Change: The first step toward transformation is acknowledging that the current way of life, characterized by the relentless pursuit of perfection and the weight of societal expectations, is unsustainable and detrimental to your overall well-being. Women who have worn the superwoman cape often arrive at this realization after experiencing moments of clarity, as discussed in the previous section. They understand that continuing down the same path will only lead to further misery, and they are willing to explore alternative approaches to life.

Summoning the Courage to Seek Help: Seeking help is an act of courage, particularly for those who have grown accustomed to shouldering their burdens alone. It involves acknowledging vulnerability and recognizing that it's okay to ask for assistance. This willingness to embrace vulnerability is a powerful display of inner strength. It demonstrates the courage to confront your limitations and seek support in the pursuit of a healthier, more balanced life.

Exploring Various Forms of Support: Women who decide to break free from the superwoman myth may explore a variety of support options to facilitate their exploration of transformation. This can include working with life coaches who provide guidance and empowerment, seeking therapy or counseling to address underlying emotional challenges, or joining support groups where they can connect with others who share similar experiences. Each of these avenues offers valuable resources for personal growth and healing.

Seeking help and embracing vulnerability is a pivotal part of the crossing toward liberation from the superwoman cape. It signifies a major shift in perspective and priorities, highlighting the grit of women who choose well-being over perfection. By acknowledging the value of seeking help and providing support and understanding, we can foster a more compassionate and inclusive society that empowers you to prioritize your mental and emotional health, ultimately allowing you to live more authentic and fulfilling lives.

Navigating the Paradigm Shift: Expert Guidance and Personal Transformation

In this chapter, we delve into the critical role that expert guidance plays in facilitating the process of breaking free from the superwoman myth. **Women who embark on this reflective voyage often find themselves at a crossroads, seeking a new way of living that prioritizes well-being, authenticity, and balance.** Coaches, therapists, mentors, and other professionals become invaluable allies, offering guidance and support as women navigate the path of personal transformation.

The Significance of Expert Guidance: Breaking free from the superwoman myth can be a daunting undertaking, as it involves challenging deeply ingrained beliefs and patterns of behavior. Expert guidance is essential because it provides women with the knowledge, tools, and emotional support they need to navigate this transformative process effectively. Coaches, therapists, and mentors are well-versed in the complexities of personal growth and can offer insights, strategies, and perspectives that empower women to make lasting changes.

Coaches as Catalysts for Change: Life coaches play a pivotal role in helping women set realistic goals, clarify their values, and design action plans that align with their newfound priorities. They serve as catalysts for change, guiding women through the process of self-discovery and empowerment. Coaches offer a safe and supportive space for women to explore their desires, confront limitations, and make intentional choices that lead to a fulfilling life.

Therapists as Healers: Therapists provide a therapeutic space where women can explore and address underlying emotional challenges and traumas that may have contributed to the adoption of the superwoman myth. They offer evidence-based therapeutic techniques to help women manage anxiety, depression, and other emotional obstacles. Therapists empower women to develop emotional resilience and self-compassion, enabling them to move forward with greater clarity and self-awareness.

Mentors as Guides: Mentors, who may have experienced their own journey of breaking free from societal expectations, offer invaluable guidance and wisdom. They serve as role models and sources of inspiration, sharing their own experiences, triumphs, and challenges. Mentors provide reassurance that the path to liberation from the superwoman myth is possible and that personal transformation is achievable through dedication and perseverance.

Empowering Women to Chart a New Course: The combined expertise of these professionals empowers women to chart a new course that aligns with their values, passions, and well-being. Together, they help women develop the toughness and self-compassion needed to overcome challenges and setbacks along the way. Expert guidance equips women with the tools to challenge limiting beliefs, set boundaries, and prioritize self-care, ultimately enabling them to live a more authentic and fulfilling life.

In conclusion, the presence of expert guidance is a cornerstone of personal transformation when breaking free from the superwoman myth. Coaches, therapists, mentors, and other professionals offer essential support, guidance, and empowerment to you as you are navigating this paradigm shift.

Their collective wisdom and expertise empower you to embrace self-compassion, set meaningful goals, and navigate the complexities of personal growth with resilience and resolve. Through their guidance, you can confidently chart a path toward a more balanced, fulfilling, and authentic way of living.

Embracing Transformation: Redefining Success and Well-Being

As a source of inspiration and empowerment, I want to encourage you to embark on a transformative adventure that redefines success and prioritizes well-being. It shines a light on the silent suffering that you may endure under the weight of the superwoman myth, offering you a path to liberation and self-empowerment. Here's an in-depth exploration:

1. Acknowledging Silent Suffering: This chapter begins by acknowledging the silent suffering that countless women experience as they strive to meet unrealistic societal expectations. It highlights the emotional toll of trying to excel in multiple roles, which often leads to anxiety, depression, and feelings of inadequacy. By shedding light on this type of agony, the words I've chosen to include in this particular chapter will validates the experiences of women and fosters a sense of understanding and empathy.

2. Celebrating Courage and Seeking Help: This chapter celebrates the courage of women who recognize the need for change and take the brave step of seeking help. It emphasizes that seeking assistance is not a sign of weakness but a powerful display of determination and commitment to well-being. By celebrating these acts of courage, this chapter seeks to inspire you to consider your own expeditions and the possibilities that lie ahead.

3. Recognizing the Transformative Power of Expert Guidance: Expert guidance, including coaching, therapy, and mentorship, plays a pivotal role in the transformative journey. This chapter underscores the importance of these professionals in providing support, guidance, and empowerment.

Expert guidance equips you with the tools and insight you need to navigate the complexities of personal growth and break free from the constraints of the superwoman myth.

4. Embracing Moments of Clarity: I encourage readers you to engage in deep self-reflection and recognize your own moments of clarity and personal growth. By doing so, you can gain a better understanding of your own strengths and the factors that have influenced your life choices. These moments of clarity serve as catalysts for change and are meant to inspire readers to embrace self-empowerment.

5. Redefining Success and Prioritizing Well-Being: Ultimately, this chapter is meant to motivate you to redefine success on your own terms and prioritize their well-being. It emphasizes that success is not solely defined by external achievements but also by inner contentment, self-acceptance, and a sense of purpose. By prioritizing well-being, you can break free from the superwoman myth and live authentically, embracing a fulfilling way of life.

Chapter 10: The Cape Escape: How You Try to Manage It All and Realize Something Has to Change
Reflective Questions

1. How has the superwoman cape impacted your emotional well-being and overall life satisfaction?
2. Can you identify moments when the weight of societal expectations became overwhelming?
3. What external catalysts or moments of clarity have you experienced that prompted you to consider a paradigm shift?
4. How comfortable are you with seeking help and embracing vulnerability in times of crisis or change?
5. What does the concept of "healing from the cape" mean to you, and how does it relate to your own life journey?

Exercise 1: Create a timeline of significant moments in your life when you felt the pressure to "do it all" and when you realized that something needed to change. Reflect on the emotions and insights associated with each moment.

Exercise 2: Identify one external catalyst or moment of clarity that stands out in your life. Write a personal narrative or reflection on how this experience shifted your perspective or led to personal growth.

"We must reject not only the stereotypes that others hold of us, but also the stereotypes that we hold of ourselves."
– Shirley Chisholm

CHAPTER II

HEALING FROM THE WEIGHT OF THE CAPE

Layla had always been the go-to person for everyone around her. As a devoted wife, a mother of two young children, and a successful marketing executive, she prided herself on her ability to juggle multiple roles effortlessly. But beneath the disguise of competence lay a woman overwhelmed by the weight of her responsibilities.

It started with subtle signs: feeling exhausted all the time, struggling to concentrate at work, and snapping at her loved ones over trivial matters. Layla brushed off these symptoms as mere byproducts of a busy life, convinced that she could power through the fatigue and stress.

However, as weeks turned into months, Layla's symptoms only worsened. She found herself struggling to get out of bed in the morning, dreading the thought of facing another hectic day. Panic attacks became a regular occurrence, leaving her feeling helpless and out of control.

It was during one particularly distressing day that Layla realized she could no longer ignore the warning signs. With trembling hands, she reached for her phone and dialed her best friend Jane's number. Through tears, Layla poured out her heart, admitting for the first time that she was struggling to cope.

Jane listened with compassion, offering a comforting presence in Layla's moment of vulnerability. With gentle encouragement, she urged Layla to seek professional help, promising her she would go along with her to her first appointment. Jane reassured Layla that there was no shame in needing support.

The following day, Layla made an appointment with a therapist specializing in burnout and stress management. It was a scary step, but Layla knew it was necessary if she ever hoped to reclaim her life and well-being.

In therapy, Layla learned the importance of self-care as a foundation for healing. She discovered that prioritizing her own needs was not selfish but essential for maintaining both her physical and emotional health. Through guided meditation, relaxation exercises, and journaling, Layla began to reconnect with herself on a deeper level, nurturing her inner strength.

The most intense revelation came in the form of redefining her values and priorities. Layla realized that she had been living her life according to society's expectations rather than her own authentic desires. She made the courageous decision to reassess her career goals, scaling back her hours at work to spend more time with her family and pursue her passion for painting.

As Layla took her first steps on her journey of healing, she discovered a newfound sense of freedom and empowerment. With each step forward, she felt the weight of the superwoman cape gradually lifting, replaced by a comforting sense of self-acceptance and inner peace. Her story serves as a testament to the transformative power of self-care, support, and redefining one's values. Through Layla's odyssey, I hope you are moved to look more closely at your own path of healing, knowing that you are not alone in your struggles. Please know that a brighter, more fulfilling future awaits you on the other side of burnout. Layla's chronicle also serves as a powerful reminder that healing is not a linear process but an exploration of self-discovery and transformation. It is a testament to the resilience of the human spirit and the capacity for growth and renewal, even in the face of adversity.

As you make your way through life, managing your daily responsibilities, you may begin feeling the cracks within your foundation. Your cape maybe tattered and not as powerful as it once was. Realize that in your most vulnerable moment is when you are open to the most change. Seek professional help and/or talk to friends within your support system. You are not alone in this lifetime, and you can definitely heal from not being able to take off the cape and bearing the weight of it.

The weight of the superwoman cape can feel suffocating at times, pressing down on you with its relentless demands for perfection in every aspect of your life. Like Layla, you may find yourself juggling multiple roles—a career professional, a devoted mother, a supportive friend—until the weight becomes too much to bear. But it's in those moments of vulnerability, when the bricks of strength begin to crack, that you have the opportunity to make real change. Seeking professional help, confiding in trusted friends, and leaning on your support system are all crucial steps in your trip toward healing.

You don't have to carry the weight of the cape alone. There are others who have walked this path before you, who understand the struggles you're facing, and who are ready to offer a helping hand or a listening ear. Healing from the superwoman myth isn't easy, but it is possible. It requires you to let go of the unrealistic expectations and societal pressures that have been weighing you down and to embrace a new way of being—one that is rooted in self-care, self-compassion, and authenticity.

You have the strength within you to break free from the superwoman myth, to redefine your values and priorities, and to live a life that is true to yourself. Trust in your resilience, trust in your support system, and trust in the process. The path to healing may be challenging, but it is also incredibly rewarding. Ultimately, healing from the weight of the superwoman cape with professional support empowers you to live with authentic power—a power that comes from within, rooted in self-awareness, self-compassion, and self-acceptance. Some days may still be challenging, but you'll learn to navigate them with grace, knowing that you have the tools and support to thrive.

Chapter 11: Healing from the Weight of the Cape
What It Takes to Begin Healing
Reflective Questions

1. How has the superwoman cape contributed to silent suffering in your life, and what emotional toll has it taken?
2. Can you relate to Layla's story or share your own experiences of hitting a breaking point due to societal pressures?
3. What are the essential steps required to embark on your healing journey?
4. How comfortable are you with seeking help and embracing vulnerability as part of the healing process?
5. In what ways can you envision your life after healing from the superwoman myth?

Exercise 1: Write a letter to your past self, offering comfort and support during a challenging time when the weight of the cape felt unbearable. Reflect on how you have grown since then.

Exercise 2: Create a vision board or collage that represents your aspirations for healing and well-being. Include images, words, and symbols that resonate with your journey.

"I am no longer accepting the things I cannot change.
I am changing the things I cannot accept."
– Angela Davis

CHAPTER 12

YOUR CAPE REDEFINED

Picture Bernadette, a judge revered for her intellect, integrity, and unwavering dedication to justice, standing at a crossroads in her life. Despite her esteemed position, she found herself weighed down by the burdensome superwoman cape she had worn for years. As a respected jurist, devoted spouse, and loving parent, Bernadette had managed her multiple roles with grace and determination. Yet, beneath the façade of competence lay a woman yearning for something deeper within herself.

The road traveled to shed the weight of the superwoman cape began with an important realization—Bernadette was exhausted—from the ceaseless pursuit of unattainable ideals, from sacrificing her own well-being for the sake of others, and from maintaining a smokescreen of perfection when she felt far from it. It was time for a change, a radical redefinition of her roles and values.

As a judge, Bernadette understood the importance of authenticity in upholding the law. She applied this principle to her personal life, questioning whether the roles she played actually reflected her true self. This introspection was liberating—she realized she had the power to redefine her roles in a way that resonated with her essence.

Bernadette then unearthed her core values: fairness, compassion, and integrity. These values became her beacon of hope, shaping her decisions and priorities both on and off the bench. No longer measuring success by external standards, Bernadette judged her actions by the extent to which they aligned with her values.

With authenticity as her compass, Bernadette embarked on the path of self-compassion. She learned to treat herself with the same fairness and compassion she dispensed in her courtroom, especially in moments of vulnerability and self-doubt. Instead of striving for perfection, Bernadette embraced her imperfections as part of what made her human.

But perhaps the most transformative aspect of Bernadette's journey was releasing the superwoman myth. She realized she didn't have to preside over every aspect of her life alone, deciding instead to view that asking for help was a sign of wisdom rather than a sign of weakness. Bernadette learned the power of setting boundaries and prioritizing self-care, recognizing that her well-being was paramount.

Standing at the threshold of her new life, Bernadette felt a sense of liberation, pride, and grace. She had shed the weight of the superwoman cape and emerged as the empowered protagonist of her own narrative. No longer defined by societal expectations, Bernadette judged herself by her own standards, living authentically and reflecting the strength that defined her.

In the end, Bernadette's story was about reclaiming her agency and authorship over her own life. She had rewritten the script, transforming the superwoman cape from a symbol of constraint to a badge of honor. Bernadette was the true hero of her own story, presiding over a life that resonated with her authentic self.

As we arrive at the final chapter of our time together, we stand at the threshold of a profound transformation—a transformation that redefines your relationship with the superwoman cape and how you perceive your roles in the diverse tapestry of life. As we reflect on the voyage that has brought us here, we recognize the challenges and triumphs of women who have navigated the superwoman myth. We've explored the societal pressures that cast shadows on self-esteem and well-being and celebrated the resilience of those who have donned the superwoman cape in unique circumstances, such as military service.

Now, as we approach the culmination of this journey, I'd like to extend an invitation to you—an invitation to reflect on your own narrative. Just as Bernadette and countless others have redefined their roles, values, and priorities, you possess the power to travel on your own exclusive path of self-discovery, healing, and empowerment. Your crossing toward self-discovery and empowerment is a continuous and evolving process. The superwoman cape may have been heavy, but now is the time to redefine it in a way that aligns with your values and well-being. Together, let's embark on this transformational voyage of self-redefinition and celebrate the strength and resilience that lies within you.

Crafting Your New Narrative: It's time to take the reins and become the author of your own story. Begin by envisioning the life you desire and truly deserve, one that resonates with your innermost self and values. To start this metamorphic process, you must consider the roles you play in both your personal and professional life.

Aligning Roles with Authenticity: The first step is to question whether your current roles align with your authentic self or if they have been shaped and constrained by the weight of societal expectations. Are you embracing these roles because they genuinely reflect who you are and what you want, or have they been defined by external pressures and perceptions? It's essential to recognize that you have the power to redefine these roles in a way that resonates with your true essence.

Exploring Your Core Values: Take time for self-reflection and consider the values that really matter to you. What are the principles and beliefs that guide your life? What brings you fulfillment, joy, and a deep sense of purpose? By identifying your core values, you can create a compass that guides your decision-making and helps you navigate the complexities of your roles with authenticity and intention. Some core values that I believe are important are: fairness, integrity, trust, service, diversity, passion, relevant, and loyalty. These values guide me on a daily basis, and I hope these are helpful in helping you determine your values, principles, and ultimately personal fulfillment.

Fulfillment and Joy: Consider the roles and responsibilities that genuinely bring you fulfillment and joy. These are the roles that align with your passions and aspirations. Recognize that you have the agency to emphasize these roles and prioritize them in your life, allowing you to cultivate a sense of contentment and satisfaction that transcends societal expectations.

A Sense of Purpose: The roles that resonate with your core values and authentic self are the ones that provide a profound sense of purpose. These roles give your life meaning and direction. As you craft your new narrative, focus on embracing these roles, infusing them with intention and meaning. Allow them to guide you toward a life that aligns with your values and aspirations.

In crafting your new narrative, you are reclaiming authorship over your life story. It's a journey of self-discovery, introspection, and empowerment. By aligning your roles with your authentic self and embracing the values that matter most to you, you are reshaping your narrative in a way that reflects your true essence, setting the stage for a more fulfilling and purpose-driven life.

Shedding the Superwoman Cape: One of the most liberating aspects of this transformative journey is the realization that you don't have to carry the weight of the superwoman cape. Recognize that the expectation to "do it all" is an unrealistic burden imposed by societal pressures, and it's not a burden you should bear—nor should anyone.

Embracing the Power of Boundaries: A fundamental step in redefining the superwoman cape is embracing the power of setting boundaries. Boundaries are not selfish; they are self-preserving. By establishing boundaries, you define what you are willing and able to take on, allowing you to protect your mental and emotional well-being. It's an act of self-respect and self-care.

Prioritizing Self-Care: Understand that self-care is not a luxury; it's a necessity. Prioritizing self-care is an act of self-compassion and self-preservation. It means recognizing that you deserve to invest time and energy in your own well-being. Whether it's taking moments of solitude, engaging in hobbies that bring you joy, or simply saying "no" when it's necessary, self-care fuels your resilience and nurtures your inner strength.

The Strength in Vulnerability: It's essential to understand that vulnerability is not a sign of weakness but a great strength that connects us to our humanity. Embracing vulnerability means acknowledging that you're not invincible, that you have limits, and that you can ask for help when needed. It's a courageous act that allows you to connect authentically with others and build genuine relationships.

Releasing the Superwoman Myth: Shedding the superwoman persona is about releasing the myth of perfection and embracing your authentic self. It's understanding that the pursuit of "doing it all" at the expense of your well-being is a futile endeavor. Real strength lies in acknowledging your vulnerabilities, setting boundaries that protect your mental and emotional health, and prioritizing self-care as an act of self-love.

Embracing an Intentional Approach: As you reformulate your superwoman cape, you'll come to incorporate a more balanced and authentic approach to life. It means recognizing that you can excel in your roles without overextending yourself, that self-care is not selfish but necessary, and that vulnerability is a beautiful facet of your humanity. By embracing these principles, you free yourself from the unrealistic expectations society imposes and step into a more empowered and authentic version of yourself.

In the process of intentionally changing your superwoman cape, you are not diminishing your strength or worth; you are reclaiming your agency and self-worth. You're seeking empowerment, self-compassion, and liberation from the constraints of societal pressures.

Seeking Support and Growth: One of the pivotal steps in redefining your superwoman cape is recognizing that you don't have to navigate this journey alone. It's perfectly okay, and indeed commendable, to seek support from various sources to aid in your transformation.

Therapeutic Guidance: Therapy can be an immensely valuable resource on your path to shedding the superwoman cape. Professional therapists offer a safe and non-judgmental space for you to explore your feelings, fears, and aspirations. Through therapy, you can gain valuable insights into the patterns and beliefs that have shaped your self-expectations. A skilled therapist can guide you in setting healthier boundaries, managing stress, and developing strategies for self-care. Therapy provides a framework for self-discovery and personal growth, empowering you to overcome the challenges that may arise.

Coaching and Mentorship: Consider engaging a coach or mentor who specializes in areas related to personal development and empowerment. Coaches and mentors can provide tailored guidance and support as you redefine your roles and values. They offer practical strategies, accountability, and a fresh perspective to help you. Whether you seek career coaching, life coaching, personal and professional development coaching, or mentorship from someone who has walked a similar path, these relationships can be instrumental in your growth and self-discovery.

Community and Like-Minded Individuals: Joining a community or support group of like-minded individuals who are also learning the importance of self-discovery can be profoundly enriching. These communities provide a sense of belonging and understanding that can be empowering and reassuring. Sharing experiences, challenges, and triumphs with others who are shedding their own superwoman capes creates a supportive network that fosters personal growth and resilience. It's a reminder that you are not alone in your quest for authenticity and well-being.

Embracing Growth Opportunities: Beyond seeking support, embrace opportunities for personal growth and self-improvement. Consider attending workshops, seminars, or educational programs that align with your interests and values. Invest in books, courses, or resources that empower you to develop new skills, foster self-awareness, and expand your horizons. Personal growth is a continuous loop, and by actively seeking growth opportunities, you enrich your life and deepen your understanding of your authentic self.

Your Cape Redefined: In this culminating phase of your journey, you are invited to craft a new narrative that celebrates your unique identity and empowers you to redefine your roles and values. It's a moment of intense transformation where you reclaim the authorship of your own story.

Celebrating Your Unique Identity: The first step in empowering redefinition is to celebrate your unique identity. Acknowledge that you are unlike anyone else, with your own set of strengths, weaknesses, passions, and aspirations. Take hold of the diversity of experiences that have shaped you and recognize that your identity is a mosaic of these experiences. Celebrate the richness of your individuality, and let it guide you in crafting a narrative that aligns with your true self.

Defining Success on Your Terms: Success is a deeply personal concept, and it should be defined on your terms, not by external standards or unrealistic expectations. Shed the notion that success equals "doing it all" and come up with a definition that reflects your values, passions, and priorities. Ask yourself what honestly matters to you and what brings you fulfillment and contentment. Let those answers inform your vision of success. Liberating yourself from the burden of societal expectations allows you to pursue success in a way that resonates with your authentic self.

Guided by Authenticity and Self-Compassion: As you embark on this journey of empowering redefinition, allow authenticity and self-compassion to be your guiding lights. Authenticity is the compass that helps you navigate life in alignment with your true self. It means making choices, setting goals, and pursuing roles that reflect your core values and beliefs. Self-compassion is the gentle companion that reminds you to treat yourself with kindness and understanding, especially in moments of vulnerability and self-discovery. Embrace these principles as you redefine your roles and values, knowing that they are essential tools for you.

The Symbol of Strength and Resilience: As we conclude this transformative adventure through the pages of *The Cape Escape: Redefining Your Superpowers*, it's crucial to recognize that the superwoman cape is not a burden to bear but a symbol of your strength. It represents your capacity to juggle multiple roles, face societal pressures, and emerge stronger and wiser. By redefining your relationship with this symbol, you elevate it from a constraining weight to a powerful emblem of your journey. You become the true superhero of your own life, grounded in authenticity and empowered to live on your terms.

In essence, "Your Cape Redefined" is the height of your exploration of self-discovery, healing, and empowerment. It's the realization that you have the capacity to craft a life that celebrates your uniqueness, defines success according to your values, and embraces authenticity and self-compassion. By doing so, you emerge as the empowered protagonist of your own story, living a life that resonates with your true self and reflecting the fortitude that defines you.

As I conclude *The Cape Escape*, please know that I am deeply honored to have accompanied you while you redefine your cape. Together, we've explored the depths of authenticity, self-compassion, and the power of releasing societal expectations. Remember, when you find yourself at a crossroads, not sure what to do, unsure of which path to take, and unclear on how to move forward in life, know that there is always another way out of the confines of the weight of the cape. You are not alone in this struggle of The Great Cape Escape. With each step you take toward intention, authenticity, and self-empowerment, may you find solace in the knowledge that your story, your resilience, and your courage to understand your cape and your power to redefine it is based on your terms. I'll leave you with a quote from Batgirl: "The world is yours to conquer, and your cape is your symbol of strength. Embrace it, own it, and soar to new heights with unwavering confidence."

Chapter 12: Your Cape Redefined
Changing How You See Your Role in All the Roles You Have to Play
Reflective Questions

1. How do you envision your life after redefining your relationship with the superwoman cape and societal expectations?

2. What roles do you currently play in your personal and professional life, and how aligned are they with your authentic self?

3. How can you craft a new, empowering narrative for yourself that celebrates your unique identity and values?

4. What steps can you take to ensure that your redefined roles and values are sustained over time?

5. How does redefining your relationship with the superwoman cape empower you to live authentically and on your terms?

Exercise 1: Craft a vision statement for your redefined life, emphasizing your values and priorities. Share this vision with a trusted friend or family member for support and accountability.

Exercise 2: Develop a concrete action plan that outlines the steps you will take to maintain your new narrative and embrace your redefined roles and values. Include specific milestones and timelines for tracking progress.

"The world is not yet ready for all that you will do!"
– Hyppolyta

ABOUT THE AUTHOR

In this groundbreaking book, *The Cape Escape*, Dr. Gigi delves into the nuanced pressures women face—pressures that often remain unspoken yet are universally experienced. She challenges you to confront the capes you've been conditioned to wear—symbols of relentless pursuit of perfection and strength—and to rediscover the authentic powers that lie beneath.

With a narrative enriched by her extensive clinical experience, profound insight, and seasoned coaching skills, Dr. Gigi offers more than just words on a page; she provides a transformative experience. She encourages you to dismantle the unrealistic expectations that overwhelm your lives, urging you to embrace your true selves with courage and grace.

The Cape Escape is not just a book; it's a journey toward self-liberation. Dr. Gigi invites you to join her in redefining what it means to be successful, to be powerful, and ultimately, to be yourself. Embrace this opportunity to shed your metaphorical cape and uncover the superpowers that have been within you all along.

Beyond these pages, Dr. Gigi extends her mission to inspire and empower through personal engagements as well as her coaching practice. She is available for book signings, where she connects with readers, shares insights, and personalizes the extremely important messages of her work. As a keynote speaker and coach, Dr. Gigi captivates audiences at empowerment conferences, weaving her clinical expertise with motivational narratives to ignite change and inspire action. Her presence at events and coaching sessions is not only about sharing knowledge; it's about creating an atmosphere of transformation and possibility.

Dr. Gigi is also the author of *Let the Marriage Begin* and *My Comfort*

Tree: A Child's Journey Through Change. These books offer insight and guidance for readers, adults to children, navigating life's transitions.

Discover more about Dr. Gigi's work and connect with her at www.personallyenriched.com and www.drgigi.com. Join her on this energizing journey, whether through the intimate experience of reading her books or by engaging with her dynamic presence at events and in coaching sessions. Together, let's embark on a path of self-discovery, fortitude, and refining your lives.

Made in the USA
Monee, IL
26 September 2024

66112270R00079